NETSUITE

SECURITY AND AUDIT FIELD MANUAL

Andy Snook,CRISC
Mark Polino,CPA.CFF.CITP
Zach Wear

NetSuite 2017.2

First published: January 2018

Published by:

Fastpath, Inc.
4093 NW Urbandale Drive
Des Moines, IA
www.gofastpath.com

Book Layout © 2014 BookDesignTemplates.com

NetSuite Security and Audit Field Manual / Andy Snook, Mark Polino, Zach Wear. – 3rd. NetSuite 2017.2

ISBN-13: **978-1985019478**

ISBN-10: **1985019477**

CREDITS

Authors

Andy Snook

Mark Polino

Zach Wear

Editor

Ann Deiterich

Reviewers

Keith Goldschmidt

Frank Vukovits

Project Coordinator

Trish Boccuti

Proofreader

Ann Deiterich

Cover

Phoenix 3 Marketing

Production Assistant

John Tuttle

ABOUT THE AUTHORS

Andy Snook is certified in Risk and Information Systems Controls (CRISC) and he sits on the Audit Advisory and Partner Advisory boards for NetSuite. Andy certified in Microsoft Dynamics and SAP as well. He has been designing audit and compliance solutions for over 15 years and has assisted with compliance projects at more than 100 companies. Under his leadership, Fastpath has grown to support more than 1,000 companies in over 30 different countries.

Andy is a speaker at many industry events, including SuiteWorld, InfoSec World, and SAP GRC. Prior to his time at Fastpath, Andy was a financial systems implementation consultant for Microsoft Dynamics and an SAP management consultant with Ernst & Young. He graduated from the University of Notre Dame with degrees in Economics and Computer Applications. Andy tweets at @snookgofast.

Mark Polino is a Certified Public Accountant (CPA) with additional certifications in information technology (CITP) and financial forensics (CFF). His work has centered on ERP systems for more than 15 years. He is the author or coauthor of nine other ERP-focused books and two novels. Mark can be found on Twitter at @mpolino.

Zach Wear is the Director of NetSuite development at Fastpath and is a certified NetSuite SuiteCloud developer. Prior to Fastpath, Zach worked at RSM, where he led an international NetSuite development team. Zach is an awesome dude, who unfortunately lives in Iowa. You can find Zach on Twitter at @ZLWear.

ACKNOWLEDGMENTS

Andy Snook:

I would like to thank all the customers who have trusted me with their problems over the years. Without that trust, I wouldn't have the expertise I share within this book.

Thanks to Jeff Soelberg who showed me the value in completing v.1, and to Mike Cassady for keeping me honest. To the rest of my Fastpath family, a guy couldn't ask for a better group of problem solvers.

To Mark Polino, thanks for finally turning this into a reality after years of my idle threats.

Thanks to Brian Taylor and Keith Goldschmidt for being weird like me.

Finally, thanks to my parents who taught me the importance of learning, to Drew and Graham who taught me the importance of teaching, and to Katie, well, there isn't enough ink and paper.

Mark Polino:

Andy Snook and I have talked about doing a book together for years and it's finally done. Thanks, Andy for making this a reality.

Thanks to Zach Wear for filling in all the stuff I didn't know. This book wouldn't have been possible without your involvement, proving again that I don't know half as much as I think I do.

Trish Boccuti, thanks for just making things happen like you always do.

Finally, a huge thanks to my wonderful wife Dara for putting up with all my book projects on topics she's definitely not interested in.

Zach Wear:

Thanks to my wife Jess and son Everett for putting up with me while I pursued my career and attained the knowledge necessary to contribute content to this book.

CONTENTS

CONVENTIONS

In this book, you'll find a number of styles of text that distinguish different kinds of information. Here are the examples of these styles and an explanation of their meaning.

 Key foundational principles for a section are indicated with a tent. Principles serve as the basecamp for security design, setup, and monitoring.

 Warnings or important notes appear with the campfire symbol. Pay attention and don't get burned.

 Tips and tricks appear with a backpack symbol. Hang on to them to make your life easier.

 Tools to make a process easier or more secure, are marked with the shovel icon. Tools can be free or paid.

The > symbol and included text indicates a cascade of menu items. For example, **File > Save** would direct the user to click on the **File** menu and then select **Save** from the menu dropdown.

New terms and **important words** are shown in bold.

FOREWORD

Managing a company's information technology environment to prevent data breaches, fraud, misstatements, and errors can be a daunting task, especially given the rapid nature of technology adoption and change. Sometimes it's hard to know where to start. Guidance in this area is often principles based, but light on application specifics, or technically focused on what boxes to check, with little mention of broader process and control principles.

Many users need a more practical, blended approach. I'm happy to see that this book works to make applying control principles more accessible to a typical user. The NetSuite Security and Auditing Field Manual is designed to help users understand sound control principles and how they might be applied in NetSuite. Fastpath have a wealth of experience in the field of audit, compliance, and controls, as well as deep NetSuite domain knowledge, which they have developed as both application development partners of NetSuite, as well as customers, themselves.

Hopefully, this book will provide a starting point for solid NetSuite security and internal controls in your organization.

Brian K. Taylor
Mountain View, CA
February 3, 2017

{0}

INTRODUCTION

Enterprise Resource Planning (ERP) systems are the foundation of modern financial management. Gartner[1] is generally credited with coining the term in 1990's and today's ERP systems represent accounting and financial management applications used by organizations around the world. ERP systems manage trillions of dollars and contain untold amounts of critical corporate information. Yet, every day seems to bring a new story of corporate fraud, theft, or manipulation. All too often the dreaded words "a weakness in internal controls" appear as the cause.

This is a book about ERP security written to help users avoid becoming a victim of those dreaded words. Audit-focused books provide the theories to good security without addressing individual products. ERP-specific books narrowly address how to activate security features, but don't cover why a setting is important to the larger security picture. Indeed, ERP-focused texts often ignore the larger security picture that exists beyond application security settings.

Our goal is to combine theory and application elements into a book with the principles of good security applied to a specific ERP system. In each section, we'll address key security and audit principles, apply those to

---

[1] "Extended ERP reborn in b-to-b," Heather Herald: InfoWorld, August 27-September 3, 2001.

NetSuite, and cover specific steps for designing, setting, and validating security.

We want this book to be the resource that people look to for application security in NetSuite. For that reason, we've chosen a field manual approach for the look and feel of this book.

We expect that users of this book will have at least some knowledge of basic application security and at least basic navigation knowledge of NetSuite.

{1}

SECURITY PRINCIPLES

Purpose of Security

Why have security in ERP systems at all? Doesn't information want to be free? Certainly, information is a remarkable escape artist, but information has value and ensuring the accuracy of information is important to validating financial statements and their underlying transactions. In short, it comes down to trust.

The information in an ERP system documents and describes financial transactions. We must be able to trust that this documentation accurately reflects the actual transaction. We also need to be able to trust that transactions were properly authorized and executed as recorded. Without being overly dramatic, the core of our financial system rests on our ability to trust financial representations made by organizations. This reliance on company financial reports leads us to Ronald Reagan's well-known quote based on a Russian proverb, "Trust, but verify."[2]

In business, we trust that any given transaction works as expected when its processed. Individually verifying every transaction as it occurs, is unreasonably expensive. Instead we implement security, compliance,

---

[2]Obront, "Doveryai, No Proveryai – Trust but verify", https://obront.wordpress.com/2011/06/06/doveryai-no-proveryai-trust-but-verify/

and control processes. Then we audit them to provide a level of assurance that they are working appropriately.

Security always requires a balance. Like a safe with no access doors, perfect security protects information from everyone, rendering the information useless in the process. Good security, compliance, and control processes are an ever-changing balancing act. Notice that in this description we don't rely on security alone. Security, compliance, and control processes work together to create layers of protection designed to compensate for potential failures. Failure in one area may be offset by a control in another section. For this reason, we've titled our six key principles for ERP security our Security Tent.

The Security Tent

Our Security Tent is made up of five poles and a surrounding canvas. The five poles are:

1. Access Review and Certification
2. Role Management
3. User Provisioning
4. Emergency Access Management
5. Monitoring

Our tent is then covered by:
6. Segregation of Duties/Risk Assessment

The Security Tent represents the core principles on which we'll base security going forward. Let's take a quick look at our tent poles.

Access Review and Certification ensures that the access granted to users is being reviewed consistently on a predetermined basis to validate that users have appropriate security access. To certify that reviews are being performed, evidence of reviews needs to be retained.

Role Management looks at the design of security roles to reduce segregation of duties conflicts and improve security administration. Managing security via roles, instead of individual user permissions, reduces the number of control points and simplifies auditing. A well-designed set of roles can be key to improving both security and security management.

User Provisioning is the process used create new users, including the process to request and approve access. User Provisioning should generally include an approval workflow, either physical or electronic, to support the creation of new users.

Emergency Access Management is a function of both Role Management and User Provisioning designed to provide users with temporary access to elevated privileges. Emergency Access Management should include approval, monitoring, and follow up to ensure that emergency access is removed after a period of time. For example, if an accounting supervisor is out on a maternity leave, the person filling in may temporarily need the same level of access as the accounting supervisor. The critical word is "temporary". There must be a mechanism to remove access when the accounting supervisor returns.

Monitoring is the ability to observe transaction activities in the system to detect segregation of duties failures and respond accordingly.

These are the poles that hold up our security tent. The canvas that ties everything together is Segregation of Duties and the associated assessment of risk.

Segregation of Duties

Segregation of Duties (SoD) is a basic internal control that attempts to ensure that no single individual has the authority to execute two or more conflicting, sensitive transactions with the potential to impact financial statements. Responsibilities should be adequately spread out or segregated among multiple users. For example, allowing a user to both create and pay a vendor creates a risk of fraudulent payments designed to benefit that user. Segregation of duties would seek to reduce this risk by assigning responsibility for each task to a different user.

A key part of segregation of duties is risk assessment and management. The complete removal of all risk is irrational, and perfect segregation of duties, even if possible, would be inherently inefficient. The goal of our security tent is not to eliminate risk, but to provide a reasonable assessment of expected risks and take measures to manage, and mitigate, those risks.

People subconsciously evaluate risks all the time. Driving a car increases the risk of being injured or killed in a car accident. Hiding in the basement and not driving would radically reduce that risk, while making life more boring. The benefits of driving typically outweigh the risks. Instead of hiding under the bed, we accept the risks and seek to reduce them with safer car designs, airbags, seat belts, driving sober, etc. Insurance doesn't reduce the risk of an accident, but it mitigates the risk of financial loss. This type of risk-based approach also works well for ERP security.

As global accounting firm EY notes in "A Risk-Based Approach to Segregation of Duties"[3]:

Ultimately, it is critical for the company to understand and assess the landscape of current conflicts, reduce them to the extent possible for a given staffing model (via remediation initiatives) and apply mitigating controls to the remaining issues. This approach does not yield zero SoD conflicts, but demonstrates that management has evaluated existing conflicts and reduced residual risk to an acceptable level through tested and controlled processes. Typically, this solution is palatable to auditors, regulators and financial reporting stakeholders alike, and promotes the awareness of risk beyond a compliance-only exercise.

Risk-Based Approach

With a risk-based approach to ERP security, high risk items are addressed first, often with more controls, increased segregation of duties, and greater scrutiny. The idea is to address the greatest risks first and with the most effort. That doesn't mean that lower risks are ignored; they just don't require the same level of controls and may be addressed later in the process.

---

[3] EY, "A Risk-Based Approach to Segregation of Duties" Insights on Governance, Risk and Compliance (May 2010)
http://www.ey.com/Publication/vwLUAssets/EY_Segregation_of_dutie
s/$FILE/EY_Segregation_of_duties.pdf

Controls

Just as all risks are not created equal, all controls are not the same either. Controls generally fall into two major categories:

- Preventative Controls
- Detective Controls

Preventative Controls are designed to keep unauthorized activities and errors from occurring. For example, appropriate role management seeks to prevent users within an ERP system from accessing features to which they have been denied permission. If a user doesn't have permission to create a check, the ERP system should prevent that user from printing a check. Preventative controls are generally preferred over detective controls, but not exclusively. If unauthorized activities or errors can be prevented, that is usually the preferred choice.

Some examples of preventative controls include:
- Segregation of Duties
- Approvals
- Authorizations
- Verifications
- Physical control of assets

Detective Controls are designed to identify unauthorized activities and errors that *have* occurred. If a user is given improper access to refund a payment, for example, a regularly scheduled review of access permission might identify the problem so that the user's access could be changed. It would not prevent the problem, but it would identify it for later correction.

Users may also see references to **Reactive Controls**. Reactive controls are designed to limit any damage from a control failure. These are the fix or the reaction to a detective control. Essentially this turns the result of a detective control into a preventative control. We've included reactive controls as a subset of detective controls.

Some examples of detective controls include:

- Reviews of Performance/Analytics
- Reconciliations
- Audits
- Physical counts (Inventory, Assets, etc.)

Even though segregation of duties is a preventative control, it overlaps the entire environment in the sense that users involved in detective controls shouldn't also be involved in the related transactions. That's why we refer to segregation of duties as the fabric covering our security tent. For example, a user with permission to deposit cash shouldn't be a part of the detective control of reconciling the related bank account.

Controls can also be **Automatic** or **Manual**. For our purposes, automatic controls (system controls) represent controls present and activated in the ERP system. For example, validating that debits equal credits before allowing posting of a journal entry is a typical automatic control. Most ERP systems prevent users from posting an unbalanced journal entry automatically. Sometimes automatic controls need to be activated. An option requiring approval of journal entries may be a common automatic control, but often there are setup requirements for this control to become active. If appropriate setup hasn't been completed, this feature isn't functioning as a control, even though it exists.

Manual controls are controls that occur outside of the system. For instance, requiring a manual review and physical signature on a printed journal entry prior to entering the data into the system is a manual control. Theoretically, it is preventative and designed to provide greater control of journal entries. Since this control manually resides outside the system, only a detective control, like a review or journal entry matching process, can validate that the preventative control is working.

Detective controls are often manual as they frequently involve a user reviewing or analyzing information. Auditors typically require some type of evidence that a manual control is being performed before relying on it. This evidence is often a contemporaneous electronic or physical signature indicating that the control activity was performed.

Finally, it's important to have a mix of controls. Automatic, preventative controls are generally preferred because they offer protection that should be hard to manipulate. With an automatic, preventative control, software prevents users from performing operations not explicitly assigned to them. An automatic detective control, like an alert that generates when a user posts their own transaction, is a helpful check on the validity of preventative controls. However, an automatic detective control only works if a manual detective control is performed to review and evaluate the information generated. In our example, a review of the alert, with evidence that the review was performed to determine if that posting was appropriate, would provide a detective control.

Manual detective controls are also important for ensuring that any manual preventative controls are being performed. This includes items like reviewing transactions for proper sign-off.

Having a single set of controls is too rigid. If those controls fail, there is nothing left to catch errors, misstatements, or fraud. A mix of control types provides a depth of defensive layers to reduce risk.

A risk-based strategy should view controls as filters where appropriate information flows through the filter while errors, misstatements, and fraud are filtered out. Picture a layered water filter where each layer subsequently filters out smaller and smaller particles until what gets through is considered clean enough to drink. It's not perfectly distilled H_2O, extremely small particles will still get through, but the water won't make people sick. Similarly, in a well-designed control environment, financial transactions may still have issues, but the issues won't be large enough to harm the business.

Mitigation

Not all conflicts can be addressed with controls inside of an ERP system. As we've discussed with manual controls, a control process may need to exist outside of the system to properly address certain risks. Also, as we've mentioned, not all conflicts can be eliminated.

Mitigation doesn't prevent or correct a conflict, instead it allows the conflict to exist and creates or identifies controls that compensate for the risk associated with the conflict. Mitigation is the acceptance of risk associated with a conflict buffered by another control. **Mitigating controls** may also be referred to as compensating controls.

For example, in a small payables department, a user who enters vouchers may also be able to change vendor addresses creating a risk of delivering of a valid check to a fraudulent address. A mitigating control would require that vendor address changes be reviewed monthly against the evidence for an address change, like a vendor address change notice. The mitigating control might not prevent the initial fraud, but it should limit the damage by identifying the improper change in a reasonable time.

Conflict Matrix

Ultimately, to get control of potential conflicts, a firm is going to need a **conflict matrix** that identifies potential conflicts, classifies the level of risk (like high, medium, and low), and identifies mitigating controls for items that can't be addressed in other ways. This is needed to set application security and identify gaps that need to be addressed. We'll deal with this more later as we get into design, but this is an important piece so don't skip it and jump right into setting up security.

Application

All of this is important when designing security for an ERP system. No system has a perfect set of automated controls and it is important to not underestimate the creativity, intentionally or unintentionally, of system users. The point of this section is to get users thinking about good internal controls as we work on the design of security for NetSuite. Keep in mind that there may be more than one way to provide the appropriate level of control, even if that requires a detective control or mitigation.

{1} Security Principles

13

{2}

SECURITY DESIGN

- Access Review and Certification
- Role Management
- User Provisioning

Here, in Chapter 2, is where all the hard work around security is really done, in the design. In this chapter, we'll look at designing good security roles. This is a key part of role management and understanding what permissions a role provides. It's also an important part of user provisioning, specifically, understanding which roles should be assigned to various users. Finally, access review and certification involves validating that security is properly assigned. This makes understanding the security design critical to reviewing and certifying access.

Principles

Security Design

Good security is intentionally designed. It doesn't happen by accident. Too often companies simply rely on default security options and try to fit their user settings and processes into the defaults. This choice almost never provides appropriate security and segregation of duties. Instead companies must do the hard work of designing security for the company's specific needs.

Designing security starts with understanding and mapping the organization's processes. A good security design includes identifying processes that are in scope, documenting those businesses processes, and then mapping them to the ERP system. Once the processes are mapped to the software, controls can be identified, both system and manual, to help design appropriate security.

The point of **process mapping** is to provide a holistic view of a specific process. This makes it more likely that companies will find holes, workarounds, and unknowns in a process that need to be fixed. Process mapping also helps ensure that items are not overlooked when designing security, and it provides a bird's eye view to help identify segregation of duties issues. The full scope of process mapping is too big for this book, but there are lots of resources out there to help with the process.

It's important to work with multiple stakeholders when identifying processes in scope. Stakeholders can include individuals from accounting, finance, operations, IT, auditing or any other area affected by a specific process. Often the mapping is for a full process, like quote to cash, but depending on the systems involved, the scope may be reduced.

 Involving auditors in the process of scoping and mapping processes is critically important.

Process Mapping

Once the scope has been determined, a useful tool for process mapping is a flowchart using swim lanes. In this tool, process flows are documented on the row belonging to their assigned role making it easy to identify where the responsibility belongs.

Responsible roles, departments, or positions appear in rows on the left. Processes flow from left to right and are shown in the associated responsibility row.

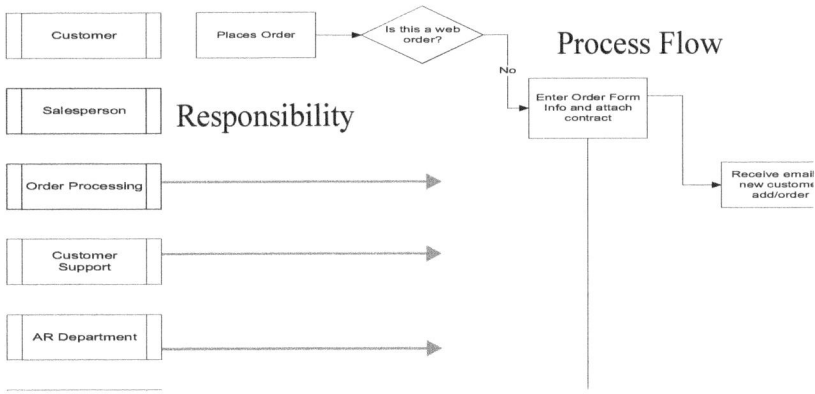

The method visually represents a process making it easy to understand. Process flows provide an opportunity to visually identify potential segregation of duties conflicts and control points. This is an area where comparing the process map to a conflict matrix helps find SoD conflicts for process corrections.

A conflict matrix would identify specific activities which create a conflict. Generically this would be something like access to create vendors and generate checks. Specifically, this might be greater than view access to specific windows in NetSuite.

Controls

Not all controls can be contained in application security. A good control environment contains a mix of controls including both automated and manual controls. Where security alone can't provide appropriate segregation of duties, other options, like workflow and scripting, can help fill the gap. Finally, mitigating controls including audit trails, reviews, and approvals are an important piece of the control environment.

After processes have been designed and diagrammed, they should be mapped to security roles. This mapping should be based on the operations being performed, not necessarily the user's title or job description. Using default roles is not recommended. Default roles aren't designed with appropriate segregation of duties in mind. Additionally, each company's situation is unique, and default roles simply won't appropriately address any given company's needs. A leading practice is to map processes to new custom roles.

Roles

In NetSuite, roles are the primary logical control. Mapping processes to roles ties security design to the application. In NetSuite, users can belong to more than one role, but only one role is active at any given time. However, since users can switch their active role, it's important to consider all the roles that an employee belongs to, and the underlying permissions, when considering appropriate segregation of duties.

NetSuite's standard roles can't be changed. They can, however, be customized, effectively copying them into new roles, and changing them. Custom roles don't have to be built from scratch. Building them using a standard or pre-existing role as a base is a recommended method from NetSuite. Standard roles in NetSuite can be inactivated to prevent users from being assigned a standard role.

When designing roles, segregation of duties should be a key consideration. Roles that have inherent segregation of duties conflicts automatically create a problem when they are assigned to a user, and inherent SoD conflicts should be avoided wherever reasonable.

For example, a role that allows a user to create bank transactions and reconcile the bank account is an inherent conflict that could allow a user to make and hide fraudulent transactions. Separating these two actions into different roles removes the inherent conflict. Users may still end up with conflicts when assigned to more than one role, but building roles with minimal conflicts at least eliminates inherent conflicts when assigning a given role.

Application

When designing security in NetSuite, it's important to understand some NetSuite security specifics. In this section, we'll dig deeper into some NetSuite security details to help the design process. In future chapters, we'll go into these items with more detail on specifically how to set them up.

Third-Party Audit Reports

As a cloud-based provider, NetSuite security is a shared responsibility between NetSuite and user companies. NetSuite is responsible for maintaining and securing the infrastructure and the database, providing system access, and managing change control for new features and upgrades, in addition to the backup and restore processes. Companies using NetSuite are responsible for user access, user security, internal controls, data access, scripting and related change management, along with maintaining a business continuity plan.

As part of its responsibility, NetSuite issues several independent, third-party, audited reports that describe the design and operating effectiveness of customer impacting controls in place within NetSuite. These reports include:

- Audited Financial Statements/SEC Filings
- ISO 27001 Certification
- AICPA SSAE 16 Type II/ ISAE 3402 (SOC1)
- Service Organization Control 2 Type II (SOC2)
- Payment Card Industry Data Security Standard (PCI-DSS)

Where such reports are not available, or where disclosure of the information in such reports would present a potential security conflict, NetSuite attempts to issue certificates, attestations of compliance, and/or point customers to their registration of compliance on government and industry authority websites and registration lists. NetSuite provides more information on each of these reports in their whitepaper "NetSuite Control Considerations for Financial Reporting"[4] available from NetSuite.

Companies using NetSuite should review the relevant reports with their auditors to determine their scope of reliance on these reports.

Overview of Responsibilities[4]

AREA	NETSUITE				CUSTOMER
	SOC 1	SOC 2	ISO 27001	PCI-DSS	
ITGC – Change Management	✓	✓	✓	✓	✓
ITGC – Logical Access	✓	✓	✓	✓	✓
ITGC – Network and DB (back-end) Security	✓	✓	✓	✓	x
ITGC – Back-up and Restoration	✓	x	x	x	✓
ITGC – BCP/Disaster Recovery	x	✓	✓	x	✓
ITGC – System Uptime and Availability	✓	x	x	x	x
ITGC - Customer Authentication Requirements (access to customer NetSuite instance/customer database)	✓	x	x	x	✓
Business Process – IT Application Controls	x	x	x	x	✓

(✓ = applies, x = does not apply)

Roles and Permissions Overview

Before designing security, it's important to have at least a basic understanding of how security works in NetSuite. Here we'll look at how NetSuite security works as part of our security design consideration. After processes have been designed and reviewed, they should be mapped to roles. In NetSuite, a role is a set of permissions with access levels. Permissions are collected into roles and roles are assigned to users, who can be employees, vendors, customers, partners.

Roles can also be assigned to contacts. Access for contacts is granted from the context of the parent customer, but the roles granted to contact records can be different from that of the parent customer.

---

[4] NetSuite, "NetSuite Control Considerations for Financial Reporting" NetSuite.com (March 2016)

Permissions govern the data and interface that users can access and are constrained by access levels. Permissions are used to define the usage of record type, tasks, and pages. One or more roles are assigned to users.

For example, the permission "Bills" provides access to payable invoices. That permission can then be constrained by an access level. A user with permission to "Bills" and an access level of "View" can't create or change payables invoices, they can only view payables information.

The access levels in NetSuite are:

- **VIEW** - User has access to view existing files only. The user cannot create new, edit existing, or delete existing files. Typically, the user can print information they can view.
- **CREATE** - User can create new and view existing files. The user cannot edit or delete existing files.
- **EDIT** - User has access to create new, view existing, and edit existing files. The user cannot delete existing files.
- **FULL** - User has access to create new files and view, edit, and delete existing files.

NetSuite provides a free Permission Usage List Worksheet via the NetSuite Help Center. This spreadsheet is intended to help with the implications of assigning specific permission or to find permission required for a specific task. Search **Permissions Documentation** in NetSuite Help to download this worksheet.

D3093		fx	View		

	A	B	C	D
1	SUBTAB	PERMISSION NAME	USAGE DESCRIPTION	MINIMUM LEVEL
2	Lists	Access to transaction numbering audit log	Allows usage of the Search Transaction Numbering Audit Log task.	View
3	Lists	Access to transaction numbering audit log	Allows usage of the Transaction Numbering Audit Log search.	View
4	Lists	Access to transaction numbering audit log	Allows usage of the Transaction Numbering Audit Log task.	View
5	Lists	Accounts	Allows usage of the Account search.	View
6	Lists	Accounts	Allows usage of the Accounts task.	View
7	Lists	Accounts	Allows usage of the Chart of Accounts task.	View
8	Lists	Accounts	Allows usage of the New Accounts task.	View
9	Lists	Accounts	Allows usage of the New Tax Control Account task.	Create
10	Lists	Accounts	Allows usage of the Search Account task.	View
11	Lists	Accounts	Allows usage of the Tax Control Account task.	View
12	Lists	Accounts	Allows usage of the Tax Control Accounts task.	View
13	Lists	Accounts	Allows viewing and editing of the Account record.	View

NetSuite's built-in security roles cannot be changed. However, they can be copied and modified. Even if a decision is made to use the security defined in a built-in role, companies are better off making an exact duplicate and using that as a custom role. This at least provides the flexibility to make changes to the role going forward. To be clear, simply copying an existing role without changes isn't a leading practice, it's a minimum expectation.

 If a standard role is used and the company later decides to change role security, the standard role will need to be unassigned from every user to whom it was granted to re-assign a new custom role. To avoid this, duplicate a role to create a new custom role and assign security to the new custom role.

Standard roles in NetSuite can and should be inactivated to prevent assigning them to users. This is useful to ensure that users are only assigned custom roles.

If a user is assigned multiple roles, only one role is active at a time. Users can switch roles to change available permissions by hovering over their login in the upper right. Available roles will drop down allowing the user to select a different role.

Restrictions

Additionally, other restrictions can be placed on specific roles, limiting a role by subsidiary, employee, department, class and location. These can be important for role design.

The subsidiaries dropdown is a OneWorld only restriction used to limit the subsidiary values that a user with this role can select for customer and vendor records, and to limit transaction, customer, and vendor record editing based on the restricted subsidiaries. If a subsidiary is not selected, then NetSuite restricts employee's access to the subsidiary assigned to an employee on the employee's record.

 Subsidiary restrictions also apply automatically to classes, departments and locations. For example: The Chicago location is assigned to subsidiary American Services and the role is restricted to American Services. Users with that role will be limited to American Services locations, like Chicago, even though no location restrictions have been set.

Restriction options for employees, departments, classes, and locations include:

- **none - no default** – There is no restriction on what can be selected. Record access is not determined by this field. A default selection does not appear.
- **none - default to own** – There is no restriction on what can be selected. Record access is not determined by this field. Fields of this type will select the user by default.
- **own, subordinate, and unassigned** – Users are restricted when selecting any of the employee, sales rep, or supervisor

fields. Users are granted access to records belonging to their supervisor hierarchy. Users may only select themselves or their subordinates.

- **own and subordinates only** – Users are restricted when selecting any of the employee, sales rep, or supervisor fields. Users are granted access to records belonging to their supervisor hierarchy except for unassigned records. Unassigned records are filtered and denied access. Users may only select themselves or their subordinates.

This is often confusing to users, so let's try an example:

Mary wants to assign an employee to a record.

Restriction Options	Mary can see records belonging to:	Mary can assign records to:
none-no default	Anyone	Anyone
none-default to own	Anyone	Anyone (default to Mary)
own, subordinates, and unassigned	Mary, her subordinates, and unassigned records	Mary and her subordinates
own and subordinates only	Mary and her subordinates	Mary and her subordinates

Additional possible restrictions on roles include:

Allow Viewing – Allows users to see but not edit data.

 For employees, Allow Viewing does not allow viewing of employee payroll or commission data. Users cannot view non-subordinate records, other than their own record, when the employee restrictions field is set to

own and subordinates only.

Do Not Restrict Employee Field – Allows users to select any employee in employee fields. For example, this would allow selection of sales rep from another team in the Sales Rep field on a customer record.

Restrict Time and Expenses – Restricts users with Track Time and Expense report permissions to their time and expenses for entry and reporting.

Sales Role – Works with employee restrictions to further restrict employees based on the Sales Rep field on records and transactions.

Support Role - Works with employee restrictions and the Customer Service and Support feature to further restrict employees based on the Assigned To field on records and transactions.

Partner Role - Works with employee restrictions and the Partner relationship management feature to further restrict partners based on the Partner field on records and transactions.

Set as Issue Role for Issue Management – Used with Issue Management to allow users to work with issues.

Set as Web Services Only Role – Designed to be used by applications that integrate with NetSuite via web services. Allows NetSuite access while disabling user interface (UI) access and privileges.

Single Sign-on Only Role – Allows NetSuite account access only through an inbound single sign-on mechanism (certificate based or Open ID)

Restrict by IP Address – Works with the IP Address Rules feature to allow access only from the IP addresses listed in **Setup > Company > Setup Tasks > Company Information**.

NetSuite provides additional information on the permissions included in standard roles via the Standard Roles Permissions Table. The easiest way to find this is to search for *Standard Roles Permissions Table* in NetSuite Help.

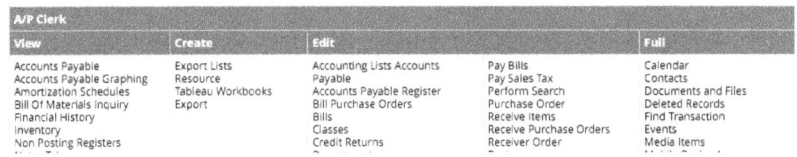

Fastpath also provide a free **NetSuite Role Permission Matrix** spreadsheet designed to assist with designing NetSuite roles. This is based on the Permission Usage List Worksheet and includes modifiable standard roles to help with security design. It's available at **http://www.gofastpath.com/netsuite-security-matrix**.

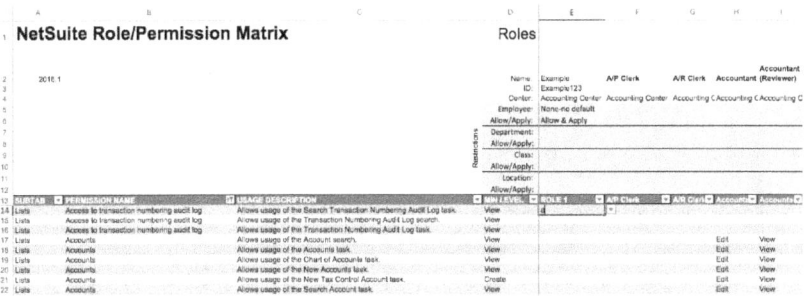

Global Permissions

Global Permissions override role-based permissions to provide increased or reduced access to specific permissions. Global Permissions were originally designed to allow temporary changes in permissions without the work of having to create additional roles.

For example, if a junior receivables clerk is hired, they might be given the Receivables Clerk role, but certain permissions might be restricted using Global Permissions during their training period. This provides an opportunity to learn, while reducing the risk of a significant mistake.

In practice, the Global Permissions feature can make it difficult to understand effective permissions granted to a user, since these override role permissions. The Global Permissions feature is optional, but it is widely used. It should be used sparingly to foster security transparency.

Administrators and Full Access Roles

The individual who signs up for a NetSuite account is automatically given the Administrator role. This is an all-powerful role and should only be given to users who require full access to all NetSuite functionality. This is usually a very small number of people.

NetSuite recommends at least two people be given the Administrator role to allow access to critical tasks in the event that one administrator is unavailable or leaves the organization. As part of security design, processes should be in place to ensure that Administrator role users receive enhanced scrutiny of their transactions.

Like other standard roles, the built-in Administrator role cannot be customized. NetSuite recommends creating and using a custom administrator role, assigning the custom role, and disabling the standard Administrator role.

The Full Access role is like the Administrator role in that it has essentially complete access, but it doesn't have control over the NetSuite account. NetSuite doesn't do a good job of documenting the differences between Full Access and Administrator in NetSuite Help. Additionally, the Show Permission Differences Between Roles functionality in NetSuite doesn't have access to the Administrator or Full Access role to show the differences. However, others[5] have attempted to document the items available to the Administrator role, but not to Full Access including:

Under **Setup > Company**
- Company Information
- Enable Features
- Rename Records/Transactions
- Auto-Generated Numbers
- General Preferences
- Printing, Fax & Email Preferences
- Convert Classes to Departments
- Convert Classes to Locations
- Delete All Data
- Administrative Notifications
- Sandbox Accounts

---

[5] CuriousRubik, "Pages That Are Restricted To Full Access Users In NetSuite" CuriousRubik.com (December 2011) http://netsuiteblogs.curiousrubik.com/blog/customization/pages-that-are-restricted-to-full-access-users-in-netsuite

Under Setup > Accounting

- Online Bill Pay
- Shipping

Under Setup > Import/Export

- Full CSV Export

Also:

- Employee records with Administrator role can only be edited by another administrator.
- The Administrator role can be used to give administrator access to other users.
- Only administrators can edit all private and public saved searches, regardless of the search owner.

An important auditing consideration for the Administrator role is that it does not show up in access reports. The standard Administrator role in NetSuite has all permissions for an account at all levels. However, in lists of roles and permission assignments, users with the Administrator role do not appear, nor does the Administrator role itself. The built-in Administrator role, as well as the Full Access role, do not show up in the list of roles for reporting, though they can be assigned to users when users are given access.

 In lists of roles and permission assignments, the Administrator and Full Access roles, and users with those roles do not appear.

The lack of visibility of the Administrator and the Full Access roles is important for audits of user access to NetSuite. An alternative role with administrator level permission can be created to minimize the number of administrators who do not show on access reports, while still providing elevated rights.

The Administrator role is a global role that applies to the entire NetSuite account.

Centers

In NetSuite, a center is a variable set of tabbed pages and permissions based on the user's assigned role. For users with related roles, a center provides the pages and links they need to do their job. For example, the Accounting Center's tabbed pages provide data and links that are relevant for accountants, bookkeepers, payroll managers, and clerks.

Centers are designed to provide a basic set of permissions common to specific areas. A role is required to have a defined center, which is set during role creation or customization. Centers function as sub-roles or common base permissions. While centers aren't as important to security design as say, understanding permissions, they are tied to roles so understanding centers is helpful when designing roles.

Additionally, centers control the way that navigation menus are organized, standard dashboards, and assignable published dashboards. When creating documentation for users, understanding that the center assigned to them controls the look and position of their navigation menus is important.

The NetSuite Help topic *Standard Centers* can provide more information on default centers.

Role Permissions Differences Report

Since NetSuite standard roles can't be modified, it's recommended to copy an existing role as a starting point when building new custom roles based on a security design. From there, permissions can be added, removed, or adjusted to match the design. The Security Role Permissions Differences report can help when deciding which role to start with. The report compares two roles and shows either all permissions in both roles, or just the differences. After security has been set, this report is also extremely useful in identifying differences between roles when auditing security. To run the Role Permissions Differences Report:

1. Select **Setup > Users/Roles > Show Role Differences.**
2. Select a **Base Role** and a **Compare To** role.

Show Permission Differences Between Roles

Cancel		Show

BASE ROLE *

03: Inside Sales ▼

COMPARE TO *

02: Engineering

03: Inside Sales

03: VP Sales

04: Purchasing

05: Manufacturing

06: Machine Shop

07: Assembly

08: Inspection

09: Shipping

3. Check the box **Only Show Differences** on the right

✔ ONLY SHOW DIFFERENCES

4. Click **Show** to display the differences.

Role Permission Differences

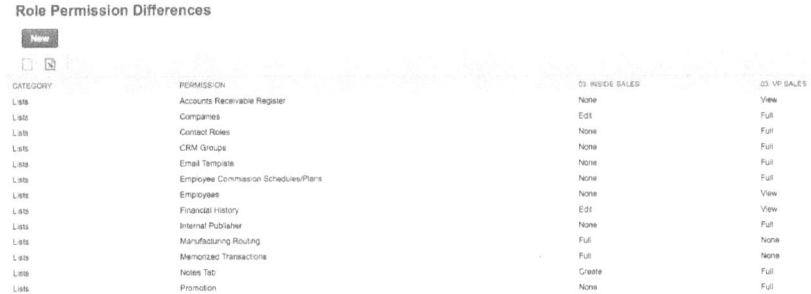

CATEGORY	PERMISSION	03: INSIDE SALES	03: VP SALES
Lists	Accounts Receivable Register	None	View
Lists	Companies	Edit	Full
Lists	Contact Roles	None	Full
Lists	CRM Groups	None	Full
Lists	Email Template	None	Full
Lists	Employee Commission Schedules/Plans	None	Full
Lists	Employees	None	View
Lists	Financial History	Edit	View
Lists	Internal Publisher	None	Full
Lists	Manufacturing Routing	Full	None
Lists	Memorized Transactions	Full	None
Lists	Notes Tab	Create	Full
Lists	Promotion	None	Full

5. The report can be exported to CSV or Excel using the corresponding buttons in the upper left under **New.**

Role Permission Differences

CATEGORY	PERMISSION	03: INSIDE SALES
Lists	Accounts Receivable Register	None
Lists	Companies	Edit
Lists	Contact Roles	None
Lists	CRM Groups	None
Lists	Email Template	None

Mapping processes and designing security is the hardest part of the security process. With a good design, the actual setup of security is easy. It might be time consuming, but all the decisions have been made. This is where the bulk of the effort should go into security.

Once a company's security design is complete, it should be reviewed and approved with a signature. This is going to be the baseline security setup. That doesn't mean that it won't change as security is tested and as processes and positions evolve over time, but it is the baseline that test security should be set to, so it needs to be approved.

{3}

ACCESS CONTROL

- Role Management
- User Provisioning

In this chapter, we'll look at managing application access for users. As we look at access control, we will get into user provisioning, the process of authorizing and adding users. We will also touch on assigning roles, a part of role management.

In the next chapter, we'll dig deeper into controlling what users can do once they have access, but here we are focused on managing user creation, removal, and connections.

Principles

Authorization

A key piece of ERP security is preventing unauthorized users from accessing the accounting application, essentially controlling the perimeter. In the case of on premise or hybrid installations, this includes controlling physical access to the server, managing certificates, configuring firewalls, and controlling network access among other activities. For hosted or cloud applications, server side security primarily rests with the application vendor. Managing server security, certificates, and infrastructure is generally the responsibility of the cloud provider.

It's important that the addition of new users and their respective security be authorized. This is a frontline control and there needs to be a process in place to authorize new users and their security roles. Fortunately, this is a process that many companies handle well.

Similarly, there needs to be a process to authorize changes to a user's access as people move into new roles and change departments. Often the change process in mid-market firms isn't as consistent as the process for new users.

Orphaned Users

Being able to demonstrate that user additions and changes were properly approved goes hand in hand with ensuring that terminated users are removed in a timely manner. Users should be terminated in the ERP system at the time the individual leaves the organization or has a change in status that would require terminating their access. Orphaned users, terminated users with active logins, represent a significant security risk. Terminated users should be inactivated rather than deleted. Deleting a user in NetSuite removes the user from system notes making it difficult, if not impossible, to identify changes made by the deleted user.

Missed notification is a major source of orphaned users. It's important that companies have a mechanism to communicate when users leave the organization. Often that mechanism is an email, but email is unreliable. Emails get missed, can end up in the junk folder, and don't provide a confirmation that the action was completed. Because of this, a regular, periodic review of active users is required.

 Identity Manager from Fastpath provides a secure portal for requesting: new user creation, modifications to existing users, and termination of users in NetSuite. The request for any of these actions is routed through an approval workflow and then automatically processed in NetSuite to provide an audit trail of requests and approvals.

Reviews

Access reviews are key controls designed to ensure that access controls are operating properly. Managers should be reviewing which users have access and confirming that only appropriate users are represented.

Access reviews should be performed on a regular basis. The schedule may vary from company to company, but access reviews should occur annually at the absolute minimum. NetSuite recommends reviews of role assignments and permissions at least quarterly[6] and we agree.

Once a well-managed and designed system of roles and permission management is established, customers may want to move to a model of only auditing role and permission changes on a quarterly basis, and performing a full audit annually.[7]

---

[6] NetSuite, "NetSuite Control Considerations for Financial Reporting" NetSuite.com (March 2016)

[7] NetSuite, "NetSuite Control Considerations for Financial Reporting" NetSuite.com (March 2016)

Additionally, it's important that companies provide evidence that the reviews are being done in a timely manner in the form of physical or electronic sign-off. These access reviews provide the detective control to mitigate the same risk as the as the preventative provisioning controls discussed above. Controlling access is a primary level of defense. Validating that access control processes are being performed, as evidenced by access reviews, provides another layer of protection.

Access Considerations

External control is important. Managing user access to a firm's ERP system is a key control, but there can be additional controls available to help provide defense in depth. For example, on premise applications may have a VPN as additional defense. The VPN provides an additional layer of access security. Cloud-based applications can also provide additional layers of defense like limiting the IP addresses that can be used to access the application. This could be used to limit employees' access to computers joined to the company's network. Another example is options to limit access from mobile devices, providing another layer of control.

The decisions that an organization makes when choosing which options to use to control access should be risk based and tied to the organization's needs. For example, firms with a highly mobile workforce, may not reasonably be able to limit access to specific IP addresses.

Related to access controls are settings like password complexity. Strong external controls can be bypassed if weak password security is allowed.

Similarly, minimizing users assigned Administrator or Full Access roles is critically important to limiting access to the system.

 Fastpath Assure for NetSuite provides tools and reports out of the box for access reviews and electronic signatures to provide evidence of those reviews.

Integrating Applications and Services

Another piece of external security is access by integrating applications or services. It's important to understand the security given to third-party applications that plug into the ERP system and ensuring that those applications have the minimum security required. It's not uncommon for integrating applications to be given Administrator level security when that isn't required. We dig deeper into integrating applications and services as part of our coverage of customizations and scripting in Chapter 6.

Application

Let's look at applying many of these ideas inside of NetSuite. In this chapter, we're just looking at the basics of access. In the next chapter, we will get deeper into specifics, especially with restrictions. More information about setup options comes later in this chapter, but to get started, let's create a user in NetSuite.

User Creation

NetSuite allows different kinds of users including:
- Employees
- Vendors

- Customers
- Partners
- Contacts

The type of user being set up limits what access can be given to a user. Once a new user has been properly authorized, they need to be set up in NetSuite. Let's start with setting up the most common type, an employee user. To setup an employee user in NetSuite:

1. Select **Lists > Employee > New.**
2. Use the default form listed under **Custom Form** or change the form based on the organization's requirements.
3. Enter the **Employee ID**. Employee ID is a required field, as indicated by the small red asterisk next to the field name. If the box indicates "**Copied From Name**" and the **Auto** box next to Employee ID is a checked, this field will auto-populate from the employee's name. If it's not checked, the administrator adding the user can type an ID directly into the Employee ID field.

The ability to customize NetSuite means that a company's specific form could be laid out differently.

4. Enter an email address for the employee in the **Email** field. Email is required as part of the user's login.
5. If applicable, select a subsidiary from the dropdown in the **Subsidiary** field.

Restricting the subsidiary the employee is related to will ensure they are unable to see results of operations, transact against, or search for data related to other areas of the business.

By default, the small number of required fields indicated with an asterisk are the minimum number of fields required to create an employee. However, customized forms may have additional required fields. Also, it's a leading practice to fill in as much available information as possible to fully document this employee user. Finally, selecting a template can help autofill information for specific types of users.

6. Select the **Access** subtab at the bottom.

7. Check the box marked **Give Access.** This is what provides access to NetSuite.

8. Check the box marked **Send Notification Email** to have NetSuite notify the user that they've been granted access.

9. Key in a password to the **Password** and **Confirm Password** fields and validate that the password meets the complexity requirements as evidenced by green checkmarks at the right.

Password complexity rules appear at the right and will check the password for compliance. We cover setting password complexity later in this chapter.

10. Check the box marked **Require Password Change on Next Login** to force the user to change their password after they've logged in. Checking this box is a leading practice in helping secure the perimeter.

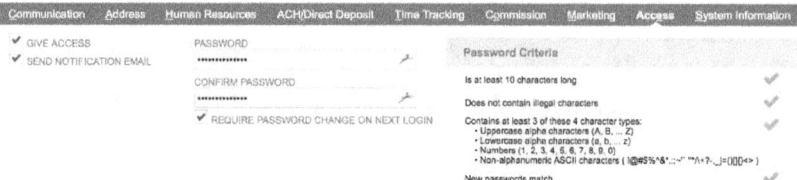

11. Below the subtab, select one or more roles to define the access granted to this user. We'll cover role setup in the next chapter.

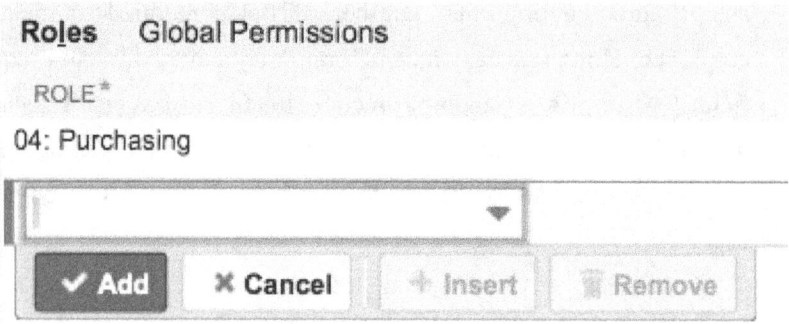

12. Click **Add** to add a role to the user.
13. Click the **Save** button or the **Save and New** dropdown next to the **Save** button to save the employee record and finalize the setup of a new employee NetSuite user.

Setting up Vendor, Customer, Contacts, and Partner users follows a similar pattern. The setup for each of these can be found at:

- Vendor – **Lists > Relationships > Vendors > New**
- Customer – **Lists > Relationships > Customers > New**
- Contacts – **Lists > Relationships > Customers > New**

- Partners – **Lists > Relationships > Partners > New**

In each case:

1. Enter at least the required fields.
2. Select the **Access** subtab.
3. Check the box marked **Give Access.** This is what provides access to NetSuite.
4. Check the box marked **Send Notification Email** to have NetSuite notify the user that they've been granted access.
5. Key in a password to the **Password** and **Confirm Password** fields and validate that the password meets the complexity requirements as evidenced by green checkmarks at the right.
6. **Check the box marked Require Password Change on Next Login.**
7. Below the subtabs, select one or more roles to define the access granted to this user. We'll cover role setup in the next chapter.
8. Click **Add** to add a role to the user.
9. Click the **Save** button or the **Save and New** dropdown next to the **Save** button to save the record and finalize the setup of a new vendor, customer, or partner NetSuite user.

Changing Users

After a user is created, there is often a need to add or change user information, including the user's role or password. To change an employee user:

1. Use **Global Search**, **Lists > Employees > Employees** or **Lists > Employees > Employees > Search** to find a specific employee.

43

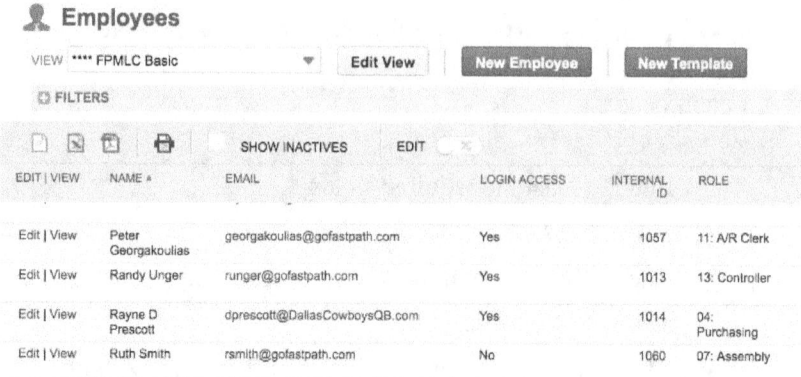

2. Select **Edit** next to the employee.

3. Make authorized changes to the employee record.

For passwords, select the **Access** subtab.

1. Enter a new password in the **Password** and **Confirm Password fields.**

2. Select the box marked **Require Password Change on Next Login.**

3. Click the **Save** button to save the record and finalize the changes.

Vendor, customer, and partner user changes work the same way. Simply find the vendor, customer, or partner record in a list, click **Edit**, make authorized changes, and save the record.

Removing User Access

It's not enough to add or change users. Removing users is a key part of controlling access, and NetSuite offers two options for removing user access. We'll look at employee users first, then vendor, customer, and partner users.

For employee users, there are two options: removing access or inactivating the user. When removing access, NetSuite recommends entering an employee termination date, unchecking the **Give Access** box and removing the user's roles. While removing roles is not strictly required, we assume this recommendation is designed to protect against the user accidently being given access at a later date. Inactivating a user retains their settings, but prevents login, and is appropriate for scenarios like a temporary employee leave.

To remove an employee's access:

1. Use **Global Search** or **Lists > Employees > Employees** and find the employee to change.
2. Click **Edit.**
3. Select the **Human Resources** subtab.
4. Enter a date in the **Termination Date** field.
5. Click the **Access** subtab.
6. Uncheck **Give Access**.
7. Select a role and click **Remove** to remove the role. Repeat this for each role.
8. If the **Global Permissions** section appears, select **Global Permissions.**
   a. Select a permission and click **Remove.**
   b. Repeat this process until all global permissions are removed. Like roles, global permission specifics are addressed in the next chapter.
9. Uncheck the box marked **Give Access**.
10. Click **Save**.

 NetSuite provides more information on handling terminated employees under the Help topic *Terminating an Employee.*

For vendor, customer, and partner users, the process is essentially the same, namely:

1. Find the vendor, customer, or partner using the appropriate list.
2. Click **Edit** next to the record.
3. Choose the **Access** subtab.
4. Uncheck **Give Access**.
5. Select each **Role** and remove it until all roles are removed.
6. If applicable, select **Global Permissions** and remove each global permission.
7. Click **Save**.

To inactivate an employee in NetSuite:

1. Use a **Global Search** or select **Lists** > **Employees** > **Employees** and find the employee to change.
2. Click **Edit.**
3. Select the **System Information** subtab.
4. Check the box marked **Inactive**.

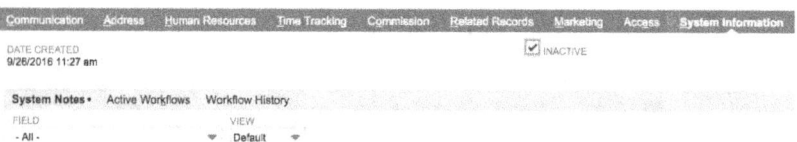

Inactivating an employee user prevents that user from appearing on lists or as choices in NetSuite. NetSuite also allows inactivating vendor, customer, and partner records.

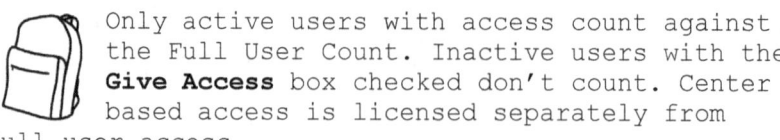

Only active users with access count against the Full User Count. Inactive users with the **Give Access** box checked don't count. Center based access is licensed separately from full user access.

Auditing NetSuite Users

As we've mentioned, eliminating orphaned users is an important control point and regular reviews of active and inactive users is a critical piece of this.

NetSuite provides reporting on users and inactive users. To see NetSuite employee users:

1. Select **Lists > Employees > Employees**.
2. Select the **Basic view**.
3. Click **Customize View**.
4. In the **Results** tab, add **Inactive** from the dropdown in the **Field** column.
5. Click **Add**.
6. Select the **Available Filters** subtab.
7. In the **Filter** section, add **Login Access** via the dropdown.

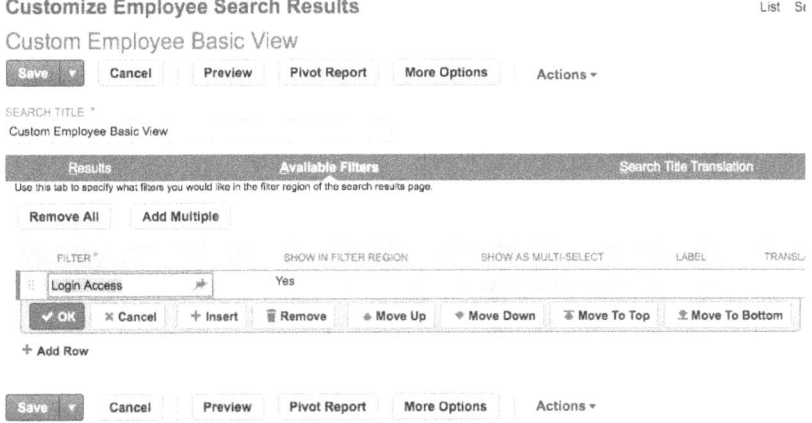

8. Click **Add**, then **Save**.

9. Click the plus sign (+) next to **Filters** if **Filters** is not already expanded.

10. Ensure that **Login Access** is set to **Yes.** This filters the report to only show employees with **Give Access** checked. Employees without NetSuite access won't show.

11. Check the box marked **Show Inactives.** This activates a checkbox to indicate if the **Inactive** box has been checked for any of these employees.

This one report can be used to confirm that the appropriate users have access and to identify inactive users with access. The resulting report can be printed or exported to CSV, Excel, or PDF using the buttons next to **Show Inactives**.

Login Audit Trail

NetSuite provides an option to review login activities to help identify potential access issues. The report is the Login Audit Trail and it comes with options for simple searches, advanced searches, and saved searches. To set up a Login Audit Trail with a simple search:

1. Select **Setup > Users/Roles > View Login Audit Trail.**

2. Optionally use the included filter boxes to limit the report. The filters include User, Role, Dates, Email Address, IP Address, and Request URL. Additionally, the report can be limited to show successful or failed logins and if a security challenge was issued.

3. Click **Submit**.

For an advanced search, check the box next to **Use Advanced Search** on the Login Trail Search page. **Advanced Search Mode** lets the user select criteria to filter on using filter fields and provides considerably more options than the base search, including filtering by formulas and join fields.

49

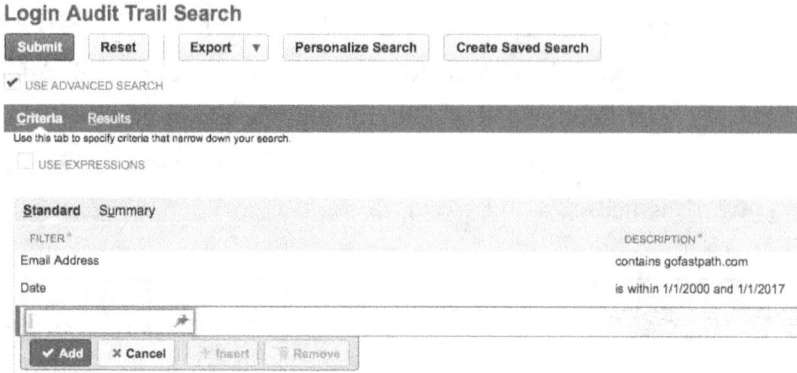

Login Audit Trail Search

Saved Searches are used throughout NetSuite. They are searches that can be defined and run repeatedly. Saved searches offer all advanced search options, and more, including defining audiences and sending emails of search results.

Selecting **Save Search** from the Login Trail Search page provides a page with advanced search options and the ability to save those options for easy access later.

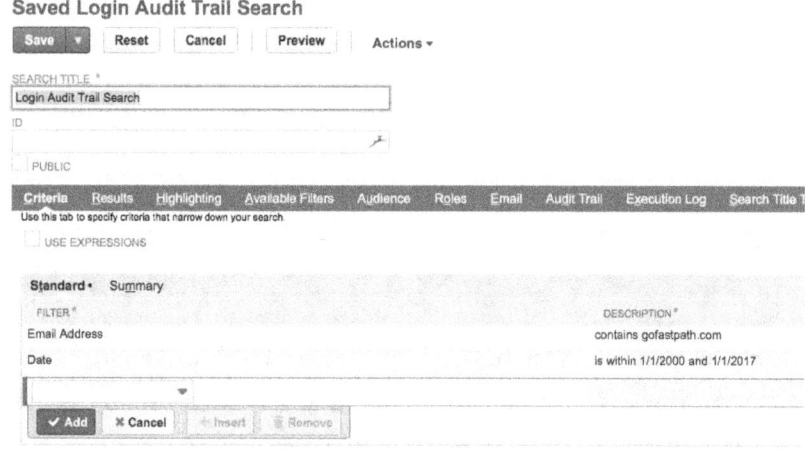

Saved Login Audit Trail Search

Password Complexity & Expiration

As part of its security fabric, NetSuite provides options for setting the complexity required for user passwords. These options are set in general preferences and the default setting is **Strong**. To change the password complexity level:

1. Navigate to **Setup > Company > Preferences > General Preferences.**
2. Make a selection under **Password Policy.**

The options for Password Policy are:
- **Strong:** minimum length of 10 characters, at least 3 of these four character types—uppercase letters, lowercase letters, numbers, non-alphanumeric ASCII characters
- **Medium:** minimum length of 8 characters, at least 2 of these four character types—uppercase letters, lowercase letters, numbers, non-alphanumeric ASCII characters
- **Weak (Not Recommended):** minimum length of 6 characters

Notice that Password Policy can affect minimum length, but not password expiration. Minimum length can also be set separately using the **Minimum Password Length** field just below **Password Policy**.

Finally, below Minimum Password Length is **Password Expiration in Days.** Setting a password expiration to require regular password changes is a leading practice and should be set in this box.

PASSWORD POLICY

Strong

MINIMUM PASSWORD LENGTH *

10

PASSWORD EXPIRATION IN DAYS

90

 Users with **View Unencrypted Credit Cards** permission must have a password length of at least 7 characters and change their password at least every 90 days. NetSuite will override and force these setting if these requirements aren't met.

In addition to these adjustable settings, there is a set of password policies that are always enforced, including:

- A prior password may never be reused.
- There must be a significant difference between a new password and the last password.
- Easy-to-guess passwords, such as common names, words, and strings like abcd123456 are prohibited.
- Non-ASCII characters are prohibited.
- The minimum password length must be at least the minimum required by the selected password policy.
- Passwords must contain the appropriate variety of character types specified by the selected password policy. Character types are:
  - o Uppercase alphabet (A, B, ... Z)
  - o Lowercase alphabet (a, b, ... z)

- o Number (1, 2, 3, 4, 5, 6, 7, 8, 9, 0
- o Non-alphanumeric ASCII characters, for example ` ~ ! @ # $ % ^ & *) ; ' [ ] " { }.

We've mentioned it before, but when a password is set or changed, the window provides instant feedback on whether the password meets NetSuite's complexity rules.

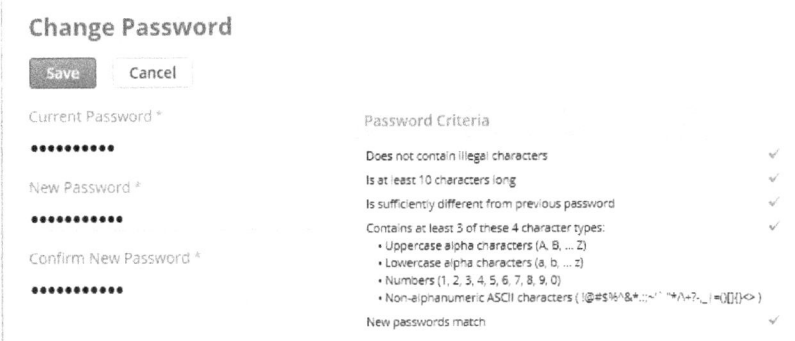

More detail on NetSuite passwords can be found by searching *NetSuite Password Requirements* in the Help section.

Security Questions

The first time a user logs into NetSuite, they are prompted to set up three security questions that can be used to verify their identity. Whenever a user logs into NetSuite from a different device or browser, they are required to answer a security question as a second form of authentication. Security questions will be asked the first time a user logs in from smartphone and after resetting or reinstalling the mobile app.

Answers to security questions aren't case sensitive. User's don't need to waste tries with different capitalizations. Users have the option to change their security questions and answers. Only the end user can update their security questions. If the user forgets their password and is unable to answer their security questions, they will need to contact their account administrator or NetSuite Support to reset their password.

Users get six attempts to correctly answer the security questions, and the user gets an email any time that their security questions are answered correctly. After the sixth failed attempt, the user and administrator are notified that the account is locked for 30 minutes. The administrator cannot unlock the account before 30 minutes, only NetSuite Support can.

The process for a user to change their security questions is:

1. Find the **Settings** portlet on the **Home Page**.
2. Select **Update Security Questions**.
3. Enter the user's current NetSuite password to allow security question changes.
4. Change questions and answers. Keep in mind these rules:
   - Each answer must be unique.
   - Each answer must be at least three characters long.
   - Answers cannot be the user's email address or password.
   - Answers are not case sensitive.
   - Answers are masked (hidden) by default. Clear the **Hide Answers** box to see the characters without the mask.
5. Click **Save**.

Update Security Questions

[Save] [Cancel]

Please select and provide answers to the 3 questions shown below. The answers to these

After successfully completing your security questions, you may reset your password by us

CURRENT PASSWORD *

QUESTION 1

What is the name of y...ite childhood friend? ▼

ANSWER 1 *

QUESTION 2

What is the middle na...of your oldest child? ▼

ANSWER 2 *

QUESTION 3

What is the name of t...g reception was held? ▼

ANSWER 3 *

✔ HIDE ANSWERS

Search *Security Questions* in NetSuite Help for additional information.

IP Restrictions

NetSuite provides an option to use IP address rules to restrict employees to specific IP addresses for accessing NetSuite. IP address restrictions are not enabled by default and need to be turned on by an administrator. IP address restrictions can be applied at the company or employee level.

To activate IP restrictions:

1. Go to **Setup > Company > Setup Tasks > Enable Features**.
2. On the **Company** subtab, in the **Access** section, check the **IP Address Rules** box.
3. Click **Save**.

NetSuite will provide the current IP address. This should be included to ensure future access.

To set up IP addresses:
1. Navigate to **Setup > Company > Company Information**.
2. Enter the addresses allowed to access NetSuite in the **Allowed IP Addresses field.**
3. Click **Save**.

This limits all users to the IP addresses available to the IP addresses set for that company. To further limit IP addresses at the employee level:

1. Select **Lists > Employees > Employees**.
2. Find the employee to restrict and select **Edit**.
3. Navigate to the **Access** tab.
4. Enter the allowed IP addresses in **IP Address Restriction**. This is a new field that is only present if IP address restrictions have been activated.

SuiteAnalytics Connect access to NetSuite does not respect IP address restriction rules. Users may be able to access NetSuite data through SuiteAnalytics Connect from IP addresses that they cannot use to access the NetSuite application directly.

User Provisioning

While user creation, modification, and removal are relatively straightforward tasks in NetSuite, controlling those tasks, and proving authorization, can be much more difficult. Typically, role and permission requests and approvals happen separately from NetSuite, via email or some other mechanism. This makes it difficult to tie requests to actions in NetSuite and ensure that operations are carried out. Workflows can be built on an employee record in NetSuite making user approvals possible, but role and permission records aren't available to workflow.

Identity Manager from Fastpath provides a user provisioning option to address this. With Identity Manager, a user makes a request for a new user and their roles, changes to a user, or termination of a user via a secure web portal. The request is routed through an approval workflow, and when the approval flow is complete, Identity Manager makes the update automatically in NetSuite.

Identity Manager tracks the request, the requester, and the approval chain for later auditing and review against changes in NetSuite. Since requested actions happen automatically once the approval chain is complete, the risk of lost requests and unauthorized changes is significantly reduced.

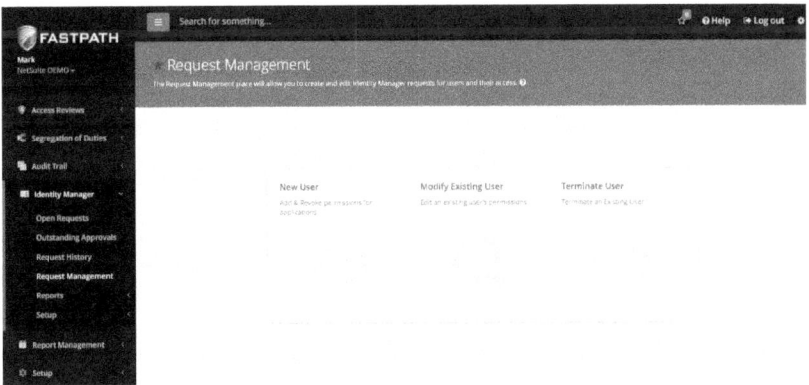

{4}

SECURITY SETUP

- Role Management
- User Provisioning
- Emergency Access Management

A solid process map and a well thought out security design significantly improve the process of building roles. With the up-front work done, administrators can focus on assigning appropriate permissions to roles and assigning roles to users, instead of trying to make security decisions on the fly during setup. In this chapter, we'll look at permissions, roles, and users in the context of preventative controls.

As we talked about before, assigning roles to users, and understanding the underlying permission, is an important part of both user provisioning and role management. We also dig into emergency access management. That is the process for managing temporary or unusual permissions.

Principles

Preventative Controls

Application security is the key preventative control in any ERP system. Security assignments with proper segregation of duties are designed to prevent misstatements, fraud, and errors before transactions are completely committed. Additional preventative controls like system user access, approval workflows, and global permissions work in concert with roles and permissions to provide a secure framework.

Roles and Least Privilege

Roles are the primary system control component. They are often the primary preventative control. As we discussed in design, ideally, they should be as free of segregation of duties conflicts as reasonably possible. Roles should also be built following the principle of least privilege, giving users just enough access to do their jobs, but not more. Good role design is usually a trade-off between security and efficiency.

In Chapter 2, we looked at documenting processes and using those processes to design roles. We then discussed mapping those roles to job functions and users. In this chapter, we're looking at moving from role design to role creation and actual assignment to users. A key piece, and one that can be difficult to get right in design, is segregation of duties. Ensuring that sufficient user separation exists in accounting processes is a central focus in reducing fraud, misstatements, and errors.

While it's important to segregate duties as much as possible in design, it can be tough to catch everything during the design phase. In particular, applying multiple roles to a user can create cross-role SoD conflicts. Part of building and applying roles is to test and review the security setup to identify conflicts that the design may have missed.

Ideally security should be set up in a test environment to validate the design. Permissions should be assigned to roles and roles applied to users in test. As we've discussed before, NetSuite strongly recommends NOT using the built-in security roles. They are unlikely to fit any specific company and cannot be modified if security needs change. Instead, standard roles should be copied to create new roles that can be modified to fit the design and later adjusted as security needs evolve.

While roles are often assigned to users when they are created, few firms spend the time to get roles right during implementation. Often companies need to revisit security roles later. In our examples, we'll be applying roles to existing users, but this process also works fine for assigning roles to new users.

Global Permissions

Global permissions in NetSuite function as an override or modifier to NetSuite roles to allow or deny permissions in addition to those permissions that accompany roles. The global permissions feature was created to address scenarios where two roles had almost identical permissions and it was cumbersome to maintain multiple roles. It was originally designed as form of temporary permission assignment but isn't inherently limited to that use case.

Global permissions operate at the employee level, not at the role level. Where role permission and global permissions conflict, global permissions take precedence, even if they are lower. Global permissions cannot be used to restrict access for a user with Administrator access.

Here are a couple of examples where global permissions might be appropriate:

- An accounts payable supervisor position needs the same permission as an accounts payable processor but with two permissions elevated to the Edit level instead of the View level. Rather than maintain two roles, Global Permissions could be used to increase permission to the Edit level for the supervisor on just those two permissions.
- A new employee is in a probationary period and their role includes permission set to the Full Access level for certain transactions, like similar employees. However, the company would like to reduce that permission to the Edit level to prevent deletions and better allow a supervisory review during the probation period. Global Permissions could be used to reduce the permission level to specific functions until the probationary period is complete.

It's important to not lose sight of the fact that the Global Permissions feature can be used to increase or decrease the permission available for specific objects. It's also important to note that while permissions are assigned to roles and roles are assigned to users, global permissions skip roles and assign or deny permission directly to individual users.

The Global Permissions feature in NetSuite can help security in several ways. Global permissions can be used to improve segregation of duties by limiting access to certain features for specific users without having to rebuild roles. Global permissions can also mitigate what might otherwise be inappropriate permissions for a specific user. However, because global permissions modify role-based security, they can make it difficult to document specifically what permission a user has access to.

 Fastpath Assure simplifies the process of understanding security by showing effective security, whether role or global permission driven, and indicating the driver behind that permission.

Emergency Access

An often-overlooked area is emergency access. It's not unusual for organizations to need temporary users, like consultants, or to temporarily provide different access when a user is out due to circumstances like vacations or leave.

Requests for temporary access should be approved and have a defined time limit. This is usually where ERP systems have problems and NetSuite is no exception. Global Permissions can be used to modify a user's access, but there is no automatic mechanism to revoke access. As part of NetSuite's Administration and Control Toolkit (ACT) SuiteSolution, they do sell a script that allows for automatic termination of temporary access to scripting folders. It works fine, but it's limited to control of scripting folders. Fastpath's Identity Manager solution provides options for approval and management of temporary access, including access removal on expiration. The use of additional options like Identity Manager from Fastpath and ACT from NetSuite provides the best path for managing emergency access in NetSuite.

Application

Copying a Role

In case the message hasn't gotten through, NetSuite strongly recommends against assigning built-in roles to users. The preferred method is to copy and modify an existing role. This is simpler than building a role from scratch, so we'll start there. In our example, we'll modify a standard role to create new custom role:

1. In NetSuite, navigate to **Setup > Users/Roles > Manage Roles**.
2. Select the standard role named **A/P Clerk**. Standard roles are marked **Standard** in the **Custom/Standard** column.
3. Click **Customize** in the **Edit** column.

4. NetSuite will open a new role with a new name. In our case the name defaults to **Custom A/P Clerk** and a number like Custom A/P Clerk 1.
5. Change the role name to **01 A/P Clerk**. Adding numbers to custom roles moves them to the top of the list of roles alphabetically. It also helps prevent accidental selection of standard roles.

Some companies prefer to put a company indicator or abbreviation at the front to indicate custom roles. Many options can work; the point is to visually distinguish between standard and custom roles.

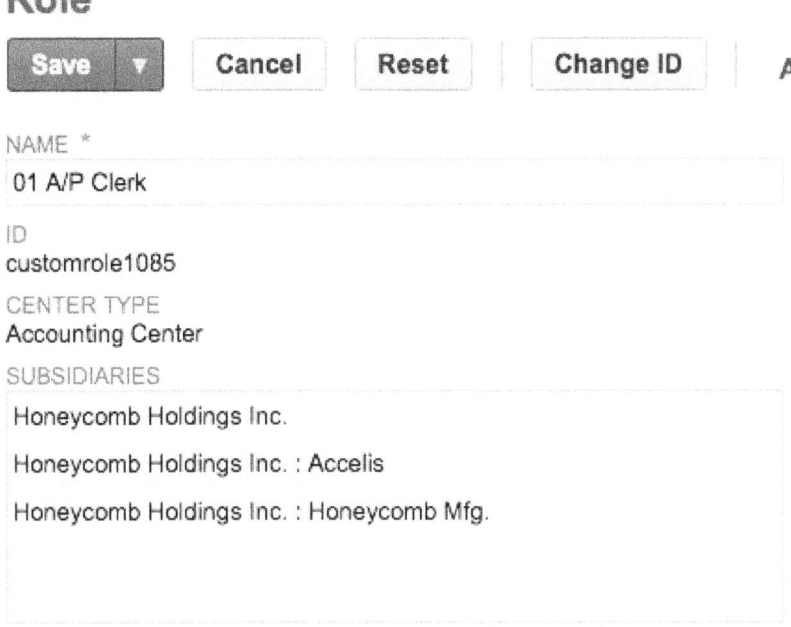

No subsidiary selection causes role to restrict by subsidiary of user.

6. If using OneWorld, optionally select a subsidiary restriction for this role under **Subsidiaries**. If one or more subsidiary restrictions are not selected, the role restricts based on the subsidiary of the user.

7. Set **Department**, **Class**, and **Location** restrictions. We covered these in design, but as a refresher, the options are:
   - **none - no default** – There is no restriction on what can be selected. Record access is not determined by this field. A default selection does not appear.

- **none - default to own** – There is no restriction on what can be selected. Record access is not determined by this field. Fields of this type will select the user by default.
- **own, subordinate, and unassigned** – Users are restricted when selecting any of the employee, sales rep, or supervisor fields. Users are granted access to records belonging to their supervisor hierarchy. Users may only select themselves or their subordinates.
- **own and subordinates only** – Users are restricted when selecting any of the employee, sales rep, or supervisor fields. Users are granted access to records belonging to their supervisor hierarchy except for unassigned records. Unassigned records are filtered and denied access. Users may only select themselves or their subordinates.

8. Set other possible restrictions. These can include:
    - **Allow Viewing** – Allows users to see but not edit data.
    - **Do Not Restrict Employee Field** – Allow users to select any employee in employee fields. For example, this would allow selection of sales rep from another team in the Sales Rep field on a customer record.
    - **Restrict Time and Expenses** – Restricts users with Track Time and Expense report permissions to their time and expense for entry and reporting.
    - **Sales Role** – Works with employee restrictions to further restrict employees based on the Sales Rep field on records and transactions.
    - **Support Role** - Works with employee restrictions and the Customer Service and Support feature to further restrict employees based on the Assigned To field on records and transactions.

- **Partner Role** - Works with employee restrictions and the Partner relationship management feature to further restrict partners based on the Partner field on records and transactions.

- **Set as Issue Role for Issue Management** – Used with Issue Management to allow users to work with issues.

- **Set as Web Services Only Role** – Designed to be used by applications that integrate with NetSuite via web services. Allows NetSuite access while disabling user interface access and privileges.

- **Single Sign-on Only Role** – Allow NetSuite account access only through an inbound single sign-on mechanism (certificate based or Open ID).

- **Restrict by IP Address** – Works with the IP Address Rules feature to allow access only from the IP addresses listed in Setup > Company > Setup Tasks > Company Information.

- **Inactive** – Select to inactivate a role.

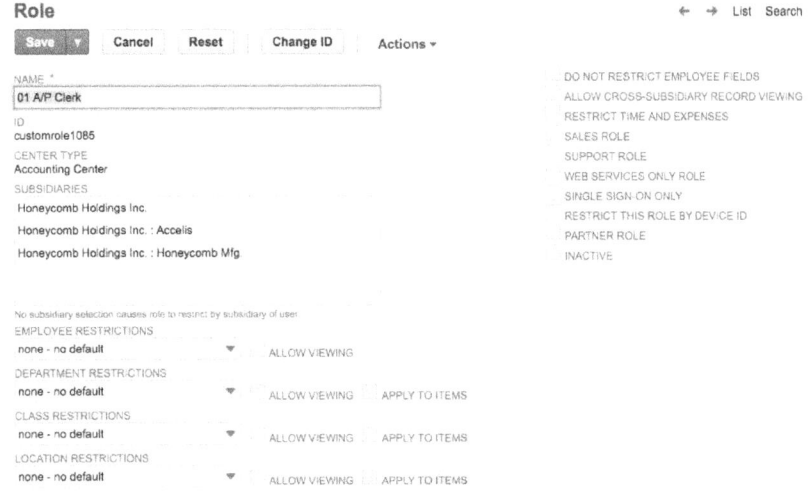

9. Set or adjust **Permissions** and **Levels** for Transactions, Reports, Lists, Setup, and Custom Records.

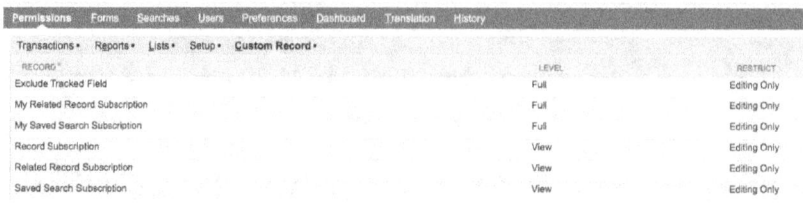

10. Optionally set default and restricted forms for Transactions, Other Records, Custom Records, CRM, Inventory Detail, Time, Item, and Entity. Default forms represent the primary form when multiple forms are available. Restricted forms limit the role to only use that form.

   • Check **Enabled** to allow access to a form.

   • Check the **Preferred** box to make this form the default. Users can still change or select a different form.

   • Check **Restricted** to make the Preferred version the only version available.

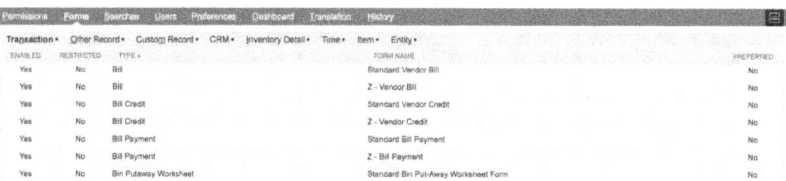

11. Click the **Searches** subtab to set saved search definitions to be used as defaults for the search forms, search results, list views, sublist views, and dashboard views available to a role. For each kind of view, the selected saved search can be set as the only one available for a record type. These selections are made by record type. Select a record type on the Standard or Custom Record subtab to do the following:

- In the **Search Form** column, select a saved search to simplify the default search form for the selected record type.
- In the **Search Results** column, select a saved search to be applied to the default global and quick search results for the selected record type.
- In the **List View** column, optionally select a saved search to be the default list view for the selected record type. To make that saved search the only list view available, check the **Restricted** box. The selection of a saved search here overrides the system default definitions.
- In the **Sublist View** column, users can select a saved search to be the default sublist view for the selected record type. To make that saved search the only sublist view available, check the **Restricted** box. The selection of a saved search here overrides the system default definitions.
- In the **Dashboard View** column, users can select a saved search to be the default view in a dashboard List portlet for the selected record type. To make that saved search the only dashboard view available, check the **Restricted** box. A record list displayed in a List portlet on the dashboard is called a dashboard view. The selection of a saved search here overrides the system default definitions.

Permissions	Forms	Searches	Users	Preferences	Dashboard	History

12. Optionally set **Preferences** for this role in the Preferences subtab. Preferences relate more to look and feel than to security restrictions. More information can found on role preferences by searching *Setting Role-Based Preferences* in NetSuite Help.

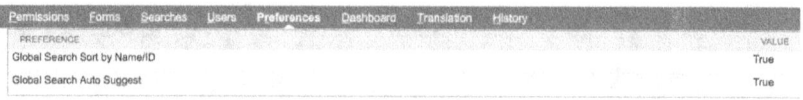

13. Optionally select a dashboard using the **Dashboard** subtab.
    - For a standard role, click the **Dashboard** subtab to select a published dashboard to be used by the role.
    - For a custom role, click the **Dashboard** subtab to view the dashboard currently published to the role.

14. Optionally, the **Translation** subtab will let a user translate the name of this role into languages that have been set up as company preferences.

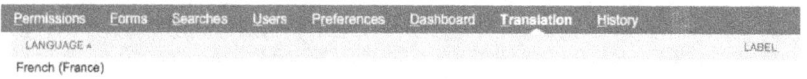

New Role

Setting up a new role from scratch is like copying a role, just a lot more work. To set up a new role:

1. In NetSuite, navigate to **Setup > Users/Roles > Manage Roles > New.**
2. Enter a name for the new role in the **Name** field.
3. Optionally enter the **ID**. If using scripting, optionally enter an ID used for this role in scripts.
4. For a new role, select the type of **Center** to base the role on. The center type sets default permissions and access levels that can be customized below. (When customizing a standard role,

the center is predefined.) We discuss centers later in this chapter.

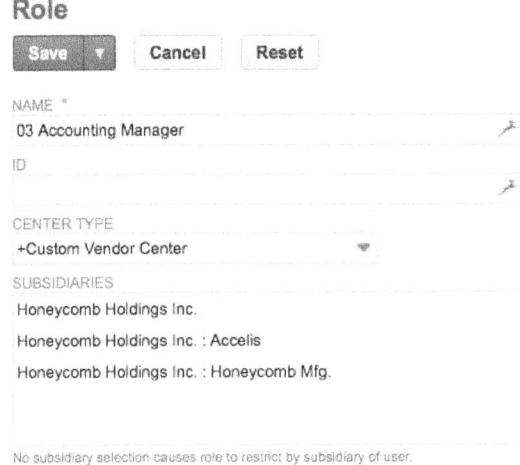

5. From here, the steps are the same as copying a role so. Start from Step 6 in the section Copying a Role.

Mass Update Permission for Multiple Roles

It can be a lot of work to update permissions, especially when reworking roles. It can be helpful to mass update permission for multiple roles. To perform this mass update:

1. Select **Lists > Mass Update > Mass Updates.**

2. Expand **Roles & Permissions** and select **Add/Edit Permissions** on **Roles**.

3. In the **Title of Action** field, enter a name for this update.

4. In the **Permission** field, select the permission to change for selected roles. It's fastest to type the start of a permission if it's known. NetSuite will prefill the dropdown list in alphabetical

order. Otherwise, click the icon next to **Permissions** to see the list.

5. In the **Level** field, choose the permission access level to apply. Select **None** to remove the permission from the selected roles.

 For custom record permissions, an administrator can select a value in the **Restrict** field to limit the selected roles' access to custom records. Search *Setting Permissions for Custom Record Types* in Help for more information about custom record permissions.

6. To limit the roles where the permission will be updated, define one or more filters on the **Criteria** subtab.

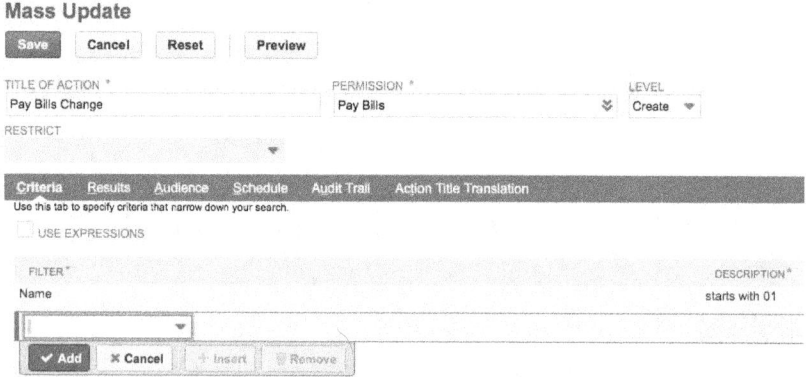

 If existing role fields do not provide needed filtering, one or more custom fields, of the **Other Custom Field** type, can be created and added to role records as filter criteria for this mass update. See *Adding Custom Role Fields to be Mass Updated Filter Criteria* in Help for more information.

7. If no filter criteria are defined, the permission change will apply to all custom roles in the account (excluding customized

Customer Center, Employee Center, Partner Center, and Vendor Center roles.)

8. Use the **Results** subtab to display options for how the mass update results are displayed.

9. Use the **Audience** subtab to define users who can run the update.

10. The **Schedule** subtab allows administrators to run the mass update on a recurring basis, but this applies more to other types of mass updates. Regularly mass updating roles isn't recommended.

11. Click **Preview** to see which records the mass update will change.

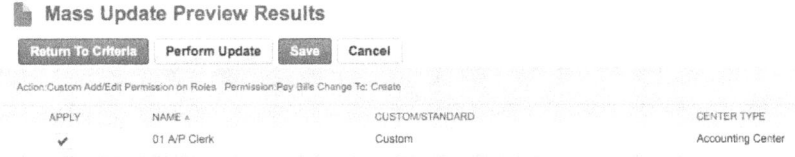

If the preview list has fewer than 1,000 entries, an **Apply** column is shown. If any record listed should not be updated, clear the box in the Apply column.

12. Optionally select **Save** to save the mass update.

13. Click **Perform Update** to complete the update.

There is no way to stop or cancel the mass update. Do not select **Perform Update** if you are not completely sure.

Assigning Roles to Users

With a good design, after roles have been properly set up, the next step is to assign roles to users. We looked at this briefly when creating new users, but since security is often adjusted or rebuilt later, we'll take a quick look again. To assign roles to a user:

1. Select **Lists > Employees > Employees**.
2. Find the employee and click **Edit.**
3. Select the **Access** subtab.
4. Select a role under the **Role** section.
5. Click **Add** to add the role.
6. Repeat for additional roles.

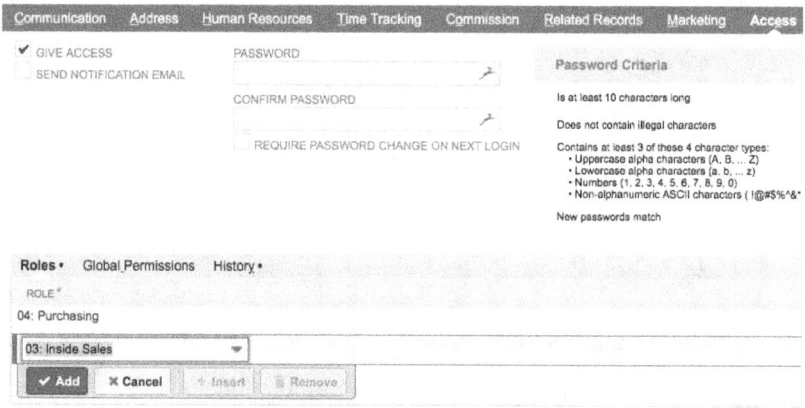

7. Use **Insert** to add another line.
8. Use **Remove** to remove a role.

Adding new roles to vendor, customer, or partner users works the same way. There is just a different starting location. The user for each of these can be found at:

*   Vendor – **Lists > Relationships > Vendors**

- Customer – **Lists > Relationships > Customers**
- Partners – **Lists > Relationships > Partners**

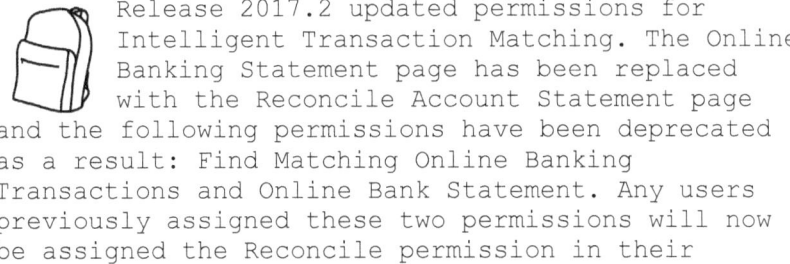 Release 2017.2 updated permissions for Intelligent Transaction Matching. The Online Banking Statement page has been replaced with the Reconcile Account Statement page and the following permissions have been deprecated as a result: Find Matching Online Banking Transactions and Online Bank Statement. Any users previously assigned these two permissions will now be assigned the Reconcile permission in their place.

In previous releases of NetSuite, time entered by a vendor was automatically approved. With 2017.2 employees can be assigned to approve vendor time on the vendor record or require vendor time approval for a given project that has the project time approval preferences defined. If no approvers have been defined for a vendor, their time will be automatically approved.

Employee Search and Employee Navigation

Release 2017.1 included two new permissions added to the Role page, on the Permissions > Lists subtab: Employee Search and Employee Navigation. For the 2017.1 release, the Employee Search and Employee Navigation permissions are automatically added to any role that has the existing Employees permission. To maintain existing behavior, the permissions should not be removed.

In Release 2017.2 additional options are available for customizing employee permission for accounts with SuitePeople enabled. These include:

- **Advanced Employee Permissions** - Employee Public, Employee Confidential, and Employee Administration. These permissions provide granular access to fields and sublists on the employee record with the ability to restrict information based on employee hierarchy, class, department, location, or subsidiary.

- **Customizable Employee Permissions** - with Advanced Employee Permissions enabled, the Employee Public, Employee Confidential, and Employee Administration permissions can be customized to include specific custom fields and sublists on the employee record.

The Employee Search permission explicitly controls the ability to search employees. Roles must have this permission to be able to search employee records.

The Employee Navigation permission gives access to the navigation menus for employees (Lists > Employees).

 The Employee Search permission is also enforced for searches using SuiteScript. For companies currently using scripts that search for employee records through the Employee Center role, these scripts will no longer function as deployed beginning with release 2017.1. For Scripts used to search employees, modify the deployments for these scripts before NetSuite is upgraded so that they execute as a role that has permission to access employee records.

When customizing roles that require employee access, add the Employees, Employee Search, and Employee Navigation permissions.

Global Permissions

Global Permissions are often confusing for users. Essentially global permissions function as an override or modifier to a specific user's role-based permission to increase or decrease an effective permission. It's important to note that global permissions apply to a USER, not to a role, and that global permissions can be used to increase or reduce a user's access to a feature. Global Permissions is an optional feature and needs to be activated. To turn on the Global Permissions feature:

1. Navigate to **Setup > Company > Enable Features**.
2. On the **Employees** tab, check the **Global Permissions** box.

Permissions

✔ GLOBAL PERMISSIONS

PROVIDE GLOBAL PERMISSIONS TO EMPLOYEES THAT APPLY TO EVERY ROLE GRANTED TO THE EMPLOYEE.

To assign global permissions to an employee:
1. Use Global Search or select **Lists > Employees > Employees**.
2. Find the employee and click **Edit.**
3. Click the **Access** subtab
4. Click the **Global Permissions** subtab.
5. Select a **Permission** from the dropdown.
6. Select a **Level** from the dropdown. (**View, Create, Edit, Full**)
7. Repeat steps 5 & 6 for any additional global permissions.
8. Click **Save**

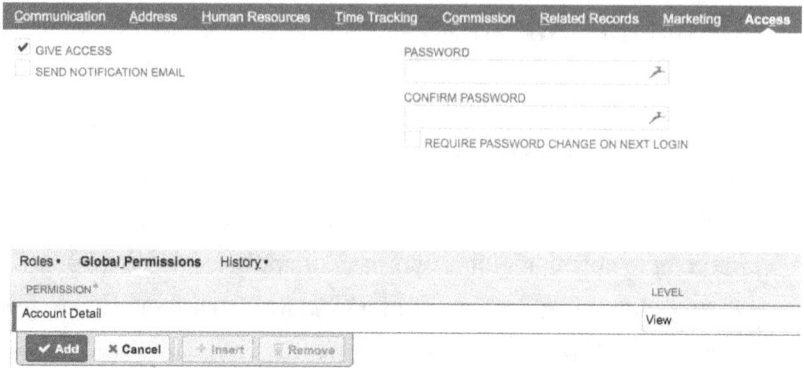

Employees need to have at least one role assigned to them. When an employee logs in, the applicable permission set is a combination of the employee's global permissions and the currently used role's permission.

If there is a conflict between an employee's role-role based permission and their assigned global permissions, global permissions take precedence, even if global permissions are at a lower level.

Mobile Device Access Permission

The next two items, Mobile Device Access Permission and Two-Factor Authentication are more related to access control. In NetSuite, however, they are managed at the role level so they're covered here. For example, a user could belong to both the A/R Clerk role and the A/R Supervisor role, but only the A/R Clerk role could have Mobile Device Access. In that case, the user would not have access to A/R Supervisor role permissions when accessing NetSuite from a mobile device.

As a cloud-based ERP system, NetSuite provides access via mobile applications, in addition to browser access. Apps for iOS and Android can provide important efficiency for remote transaction processing and reporting. Mobile Device Access also creates a risk of unauthorized access since mobile devices may be lost or misplaced. By default, in NetSuite, Mobile Device Access is enabled for all roles except:

- Custom roles
- System Administrator
- Administrator
- Full Access

 Creating a custom role by copying a standard role copies over Mobile Device Access permission as well.

Mobile Device Access permission can be granted to custom roles. Administrator and Full Access roles cannot be granted Mobile Device Access. Administrators who need mobile access can assign themselves a custom role with Mobile Device Access enabled.

To add Mobile Device Access permission to a role:
1. Go to **Setup > Users/Roles > User Management > Manage Roles**.
2. Click **Edit** or **Customize** next to the relevant role.
3. Select the **Permissions** tab.
4. Click the **Setup** subtab.
5. In the dropdown menu, select **Mobile Device Access. Full** is the only **Level** option.
6. Click **Save.**

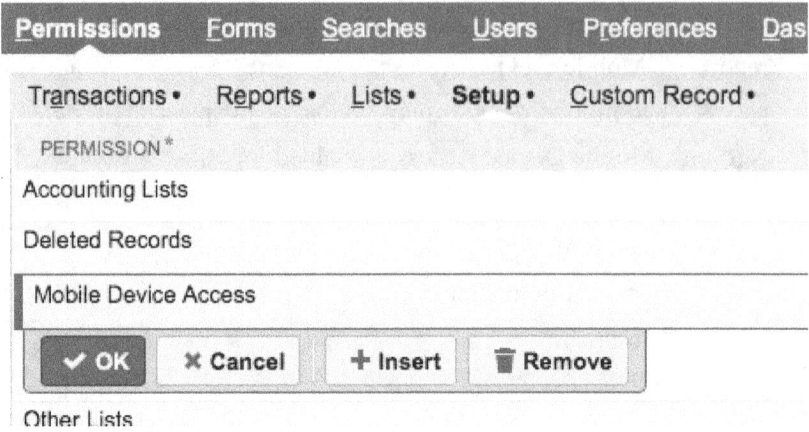

To add Mobile Device Access permission for a User:

1. Select to **Setup > Users/Roles > User Management > Manage Users.**

2. Select the relevant user and click **Edit.**

3. Click the **Access** subtab.

4. Click the **Global Permissions** subtab.

5. In the dropdown menu, select **Mobile Device Access. Full** is the only **Level** option.

6. Click **Save.**

 For security reasons, NetSuite does NOT recommend applying Mobile Device Access permission directly to a user. This permission should be applied via a role.

Two-Factor Authentication

Two-factor authentication (2FA) provides an additional level of security for logging in to NetSuite. 2FA is designed to help protect against unauthorized access to data and requires that users log in using:

1. Something they know like their email address and existing NetSuite password.
2. Something they have like a secure token that generates a time-based one-time password (OTP) for each login.

With Version 2017 Release 1, NetSuite adds use of an authenticator application to its two different types of 2FA, specifically:

- Two-Factor Authentication by phone or authenticator app. This uses SMS or an authenticator app like Google Authenticator or Microsoft Authenticator to generate the time-based one-time password.
- Two-Factor Authentication using RSA SecurID hardware and software tokens.

Both types of 2FA can be used simultaneously in a single account. The two types are similar, but different procedures are required for each type.

2FA by phone or authenticator app is automatically available in all NetSuite accounts. No special setup or enabling of features is required. Account administrators (or other users with the permission Two-Factor Authentication base) must designate roles for 2FA by phone/authenticator, and users with these roles must set up their mobile phone numbers and authentication applications in NetSuite. This is required to receive the 2FA code. Some of the benefits of 2FA by SMS include:

- No special licensing is required.
- No special tokens are required.
- Access is supported for the NetSuite UI and NetSuite Mobile applications.

- Little maintenance is required of administrators. After being assigned to a 2FA authentication required role, users configure their own settings and manage their own devices in NetSuite.

- Works with all non-customer center roles, including contacts.

- The user's 2FA settings are shared across all NetSuite accounts and for all companies to which they have access.

- There are two authentication options available for users, and users can switch between these options when they log in:
  o The 2FA by Authenticator App option is recommended as the primary authentication method because it is always available. Even if a user cannot receive a text message (SMS) or a voice call, the authenticator app can generate a verification code. Currently supported third party authenticator apps include:
    - Google Authenticator
    - Microsoft Authenticator
    - OKTA Verify
  o The 2FA by Phone option lets users specify their preferred delivery method for verification codes: Text message (SMS) or voice call. Users only need to set up their phone number in NetSuite and specify how they prefer to receive verification codes.

Access to the 2FA using RSA Tokens feature requires purchasing the Two-Factor Authentication module from NetSuite. After this purchase, a designated number of 2FA licenses are provisioned to the NetSuite account. Account administrators (or other users with the permission Two-Factor Authentication) must manage the RSA tokens in NetSuite.

Search *About 2FA Using RSA Tokens* for more details on using RSA tokens with NetSuite.

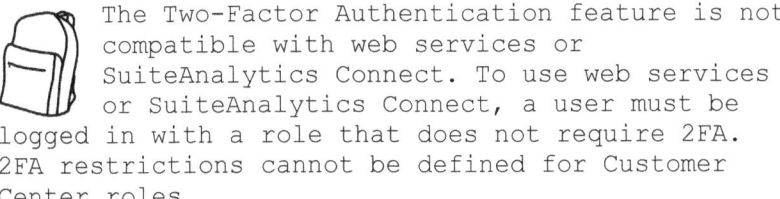 The Two-Factor Authentication feature is not compatible with web services or SuiteAnalytics Connect. To use web services or SuiteAnalytics Connect, a user must be logged in with a role that does not require 2FA. 2FA restrictions cannot be defined for Customer Center roles.

For our example, we'll use 2FA via SMS. To add 2FA to a role:

1. Go to **Setup > Users/Roles > Two-Factor Authentication > Two-Factor Authentication Roles (Administrator).**

2. For roles that require 2FA, select the type of authentication (RSA or SMS) in the **Two-Factor Authentication Required** column.

A single 2FA role can be designated as either RSA or SMS, but not both. For example, to have a role that has both SMS and RSA capabilities, make a copy of the role and designate one as **SMS authentication required** and designate the copy as **RSA token authentication required**.

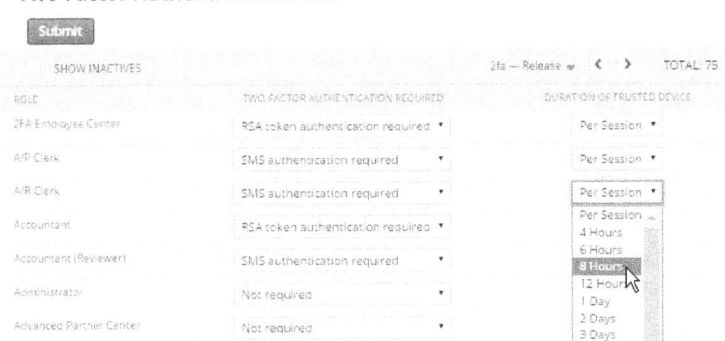

3. In the **Duration of Trusted Device** column, accept the default (Per Session) or select the length of time before a device marked by the user as trusted will be subject to a two-factor authentication request.

4. Click **Submit**.

 2FA roles designated as RSA token authentication required roles are accessible only to users with associated tokens. Before tokens can be associated with users, token information must be uploaded into NetSuite. See *Uploading RSA Token Information* in NetSuite Help.

Web Services

Web services are Extensible Markup Language (XML) applications mapped to programs, objects, databases, or complex business functions. They utilize a standardized XML messaging system to send or receive requests to authorized parties over the internet. Web services are used by application to securely interact with NetSuite.

In NetSuite, a user's role can be designated as **Web Services Only**. When a user logs in with a role that has been designated as Web Services Only, validation is performed to ensure that the user is logging in through web services and not through the UI.

 An account must have the Web Services feature enabled for the Web Services Only check box to appear. Search *Enabling the Web Services Feature* in NetSuite Help for steps on enabling this feature.

The Web Services Only role increases the security of an integrated application by prohibiting user interaction with NetSuite via the user interface. It also prevents users from accessing the system with permissions and privileges that are specifically created for a web services application.

For example, a web services application may require that certain employees have write access to several records. However, the company wants to prohibit the employees from being able to edit these records directly from within the NetSuite UI. Assigning the Web Services Only role to specified employees allows the employees to log in to NetSuite and access the application through an application using web services; however, the employees cannot switch to their other roles within the system and write/edit/delete data-sensitive records.

 The Web Services Only role does not appear in the Change Role dropdown list. Therefore, users cannot change their roles from their original UI login role to their Web Services Only role from within the UI.

To designate a role as Web Services Only:
1. Click **Setup > Users/Roles > Manage Roles**.
2. On the **Manage Roles** list page, locate the role to set as **Web Services Only.**
3. Click the corresponding **Edit** or **Customize** link.
4. Check the **Web Services Only Role** box.
5. Click **Save**.

A role should not be designated as **Web Services Only** until the developers building and testing the integrated application have completed the application. Waiting to designate a role as **Web Services Only** allows developers to test the permissions for the role that is designed specifically for an integrated application without fear of inappropriate user access. After the development and testing is complete, the developer can set the **Web Services Only** role to TRUE for a specified role. This will prevent users with this role from accessing the UI with this set of permissions and privileges.

Centers

For each user, NetSuite shows a variable set of tabbed pages, called a center, based on the user's assigned role. Each center provides a set of pages and links users need to do their job for users with related roles.

Centers are attached to NetSuite roles. Copied roles inherit their center from the source role. New roles require selecting a center.

Role

| Save ▼ | Cancel | Reset | Change ID | A |

NAME *

01 A/P Clerk

ID
customrole1085

CENTER TYPE
Accounting Center

When a user logs in, the system determines the user's default assigned role and displays the associated center. If a user has multiple assigned roles, NetSuite provides a list of them under the dropdown arrow in the upper right corner that can be used to change roles. When a user changes roles, the interface refreshes to display a different center as needed.

NetSuite includes several standard centers. Each standard center is designed to make the most-used links easy to find for the roles that use that center. For example, the Accounting Center's tabbed pages provide data and links that are relevant for accountants, bookkeepers, payroll managers, and clerks.

Each tab contains links to transactions, lists, and setup pages. The links that appear are based on the user's role and the permissions the role is granted. For example, users assigned to the Sales Rep role would see different links on the Forecast tab than users with the Sales Administrator role because of permissions granted to each role. However, both roles share the Sales Center.

It's important to note that while centers are assigned via roles, they are just a collection of permissions, so access to anything in a center is still controlled by the user's permission assignment.

Pay careful attention to the center type assigned to each role. This detail controls the way NetSuite's navigation menus are organized, the standard dashboards that show with this role, and the published dashboards that can be assigned to this role. When a dashboard is published, only roles with that center type will be able to use the dashboard.

This is also important when creating documentation for users since navigation menus are organized differently for each center. Custom centers can also be created. More information is available by searching *Centers* in NetSuite Help.

Special Roles

NetSuite includes a couple of special roles. These roles appear when assigning roles to users. They don't show up when managing roles. These two special roles are Administrator and Full Access. At least one user must be assigned as an administrator. The first user to sign up for NetSuite starts out with the Administrator role. NetSuite recommends giving at least two users Administrative rights to ensure that administrator level tasks can be performed if one of the users is unavailable.

 The Administrator role has **all** permissions available in a company's NetSuite account at **all** levels. Users assigned the Administrator role should receive enhanced scrutiny of their transactions via audit trails in system notes.

The Administrator role is a critical role and assignment of this role should be severely restricted. As with other standard roles, the standard Administrator role cannot be customized. NetSuite recommends creating and using a custom Administrator role rather than using the standard role.

 An important auditing consideration for the Administrator role is that it does not show up in access reports. In lists of roles and permission assignments, users with the Administrator or Full Access roles do not appear, nor do the Administrator or Full Access roles themselves appear. The built-in Administrator role, as well as the Full Access role, also do not show up in the list of roles for reporting.

NetSuite continues to move permissions out of the Administrator role so that fewer activities require Administrator permissions. Search

NetSuite Help for *Separated Administrator Permissions* for the latest list.

The Full Access role is like the Administrator role. It has all the permissions of the Administrator role but without the ability to delete the account. It is recommended that the Full Access role be treated the same way as the Administrator role with minimal or no users assigned to it and additional scrutiny of operations performed by Full Access users.

Emergency Access

Another important consideration is emergency access. This usually comes in one of two forms, temporary users and temporary permissions. Temporary users need access for a period of time. This often includes consultants or temporary employees who wouldn't otherwise have access to NetSuite. NetSuite doesn't really have a mechanism to address temporary users, so we'll look at a third-party option. Temporary permissions represent elevated or additional permission in NetSuite for a defined period of time. Usually this is needed when a user is temporarily performing new or additional functions due to vacations, leave, or interim assignments. The Global Permissions feature was originally designed to help with this, but critically, it lacks an expiration option to remove additional access at a defined time.

With NetSuite's lack of real options around emergency access, Fastpath's Identity Manager tool becomes an important part of the security process. We saw earlier that Identity Manager can securely manage employee creation, changes, and removals via a workflow approval process. As part of that functionality, Identity Manager can be used to set date/time restrictions for NetSuite users when temporary users are required. Identity Manager can also be used to set date/time restrictions on roles or global permissions to address the need for temporary permissions.

All of this flows through an approval workflow. Once approved, temporary users or permissions are applied in NetSuite. The user or permission access is only available during the date and time frame set. Identity manager automatically removes the user, role, or global permission once the expiration date and time pass.

Testing

Testing security changes in a test or sandbox environment is a leading practice and this applies to NetSuite as well. Security should be tested in a sandbox environment prior to using new roles and permissions in production. Fortunately, the NetSuite bundle feature allows companies to copy their sandbox roles to production, saving time and reducing data entry errors.

Part of the challenge with testing is determining what permissions users have. As we looked at in design, NetSuite offers an option to show role permission differences in **Setup > Users/Roles > Show Role Differences.** But this only explains differences in roles, it doesn't necessarily show what a user can do, especially since a user can belong to multiple roles.

Determining what a user can do is important for reviewing segregation of duties. This can be difficult to do in NetSuite. A lot can be done with saved searches, but it's still a lot of comparing users, roles, and permissions with a segregation of duties ruleset that would need to exist separately from NetSuite. There is another option. Fastpath's Assure tool includes a prebuilt, customizable ruleset designed for NetSuite to show segregation of duties conflicts within roles and across roles. This makes it easy to find and fix SoD issues in the test environment before pushing security to production, and it makes it easy to monitor production over time to ensure that new conflicts aren't being created.

{5}

OTHER CONTROLS & MITIGATION

- Role Management
- User Provisioning
- Monitoring

It never seems to be possible to fit appropriate segregation of duties into application security. Perfect preventative controls are both inefficient and rigid. The use of other system controls and detective controls can provide additional layers of flexible security.

In this chapter, we'll dig into some controls and mitigation options beyond basic application security. Mitigation is used to address shortcomings in role management and user provisioning provided through application security. Often mitigation involves monitoring and reviewing transactions through tools like audit trails, that we'll look at in this chapter.

Mitigation

Mitigation doesn't correct a conflict, instead it allows the conflict to exist and creates or identifies other controls that compensate for the risk of excessive access. When a firm mitigates an SoD conflict, it accepts the risk associated with a conflict and attempts to compensate via the use of other controls. These other controls can be other application controls, IT controls, or manual control operations.

Common mitigation and detective control options include items like approvals and reviews. A key piece of any detective control is evidence that the control is being performed. For example, if a control is that journal entries need to be approved before posting, there needs to be evidence of an approval. This might be a physical signature, an electronic signature, an email, or other proof, but there needs to be something.

Often other features in an application can be used to fill in control gaps and mitigate risks. Features like workflow and approvals can be used to break up a process where other SoD options might not be practical. Audit trail features are useful for change reviews as part of a mitigation process. Likewise, reconciliations are important for identifying and fixing errors, and ideally, preventing them in the future. Reporting in many forms, when combined with related reviews, are a core detective control, but auditors only tend to rely on them when there is evidence that reports are truly being reviewed.

A company's SoD matrix and the map connecting processes to application roles are critical to identifying risks that are not addressed by application security. It also important to remember that not all risks are created equal, and critical operations for one company may be irrelevant to another. Identifying and focusing on critical access items is an important way to simplify reviews and focus them on items important to the organization.

Once an organization is left with processes that include SoD conflicts, the next step is to identify options to adjust processes, apply detective controls, or find other mitigation options.

For example, a common issue in small payables departments is that payables users have the right to create a vendor and enter a vendor invoice. This opens a risk of redirecting payments to a fake vendor. It's often hard to segregate vendor creation and vendor invoice entry in smaller organizations. Common mitigation options would include using a workflow for approval of new vendors, or using a review process where another user who is uninvolved in the operation reviews a report or audit trail of new vendors against invoices and invoice approvals to validate the vendor's authenticity.

In the Application section of this chapter, we'll look at some options to assist with setting up detective controls and mitigating SoD conflicts in NetSuite.

Application

Workflow

NetSuite's built-in workflow solution, branded as SuiteFlow, is used to create and execute workflows in NetSuite. A workflow is the definition of a custom business process for a record in NetSuite. Workflows can include things like transaction approval, record management, and lead nurturing.

Workflows are defined for a specific record type and contain the stages, or states, of a record as it moves through a business process. At each stage, a workflow defines the related actions to be performed. This includes things like sending an email or adding buttons to a record form before the workflow moves to the next step. The actions and transitions can contain conditions that must be met before the actions or transitions execute.

NetSuite starts an instance of a workflow on a record, and a record transitions between states in a workflow based on specific triggers. Triggers are events that occur when records are viewed, created, or updated. NetSuite can also run workflow instances on records based on a schedule.

The Workflow Manager Interface in SuiteFlow is used to create and edit workflows. Below is an example of a sample approval business process for an estimate:

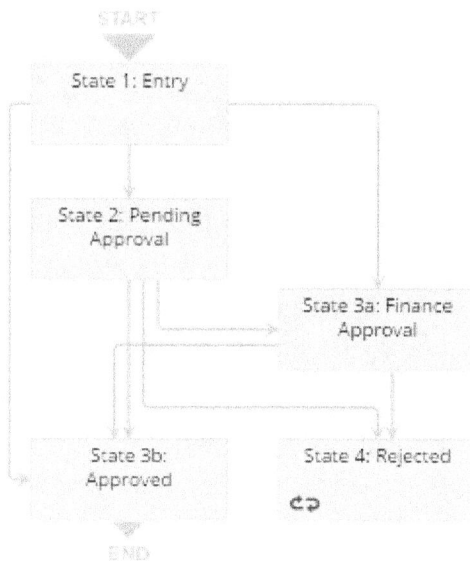

In this example, a sales rep creates an Estimate record. SuiteFlow initiates an instance of the approval workflow to automate the approval process for the estimate. Workflow actions and conditions on each state determine how the estimate transitions through the approval process.

Enabling SuiteFlow

To create or run a NetSuite workflow, administrators must enable the SuiteFlow feature. To activate this feature,

1. Go to **Setup > Company > Enable Features**.
2. On the **SuiteCloud** tab, select the **SuiteFlow** box, click **Save.**

 Enabling SuiteFlow may trigger a series of prompts to enable Client and Server SuiteScript. Do not turn off any of these features after they are enabled.

Workflows from Templates

Workflows can be a complicated topic. We'll cover workflows here, but we won't delve into them deeply. Since workflows often function as mitigating controls on top of security, there is a virtually unlimited set of potential options and NetSuite provides a lot of assistance for workflows in the Help area. In addition, NetSuite also provides some workflow templates out of the box to make things easier. Even more important, three of the four default templates are approval workflows designed to assist with mitigating risk.

The three out-of-the-box approval templates are:

- Journal Entry Basic Approval
- Purchase Order Basic Approval
- Sales Order Basic Approval

To build a workflow using the Journal Entry Basic Approval template:

1. Select **Customization > Workflow> Workflows > New**.
2. On the left, select **From Template.**

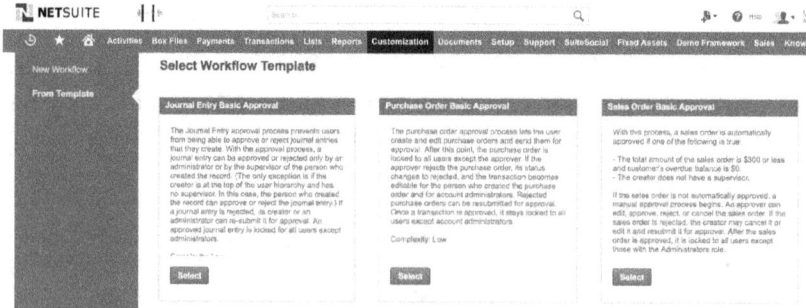

3. In the center under **Select Workflow Template,** click **Select** in the **Journal Entry Basic Approval** box.

4. A basic workflow is created with steps for Initiation, Pending Approval, Approval, and Rejection. Click **Done Editing** to create the workflow.

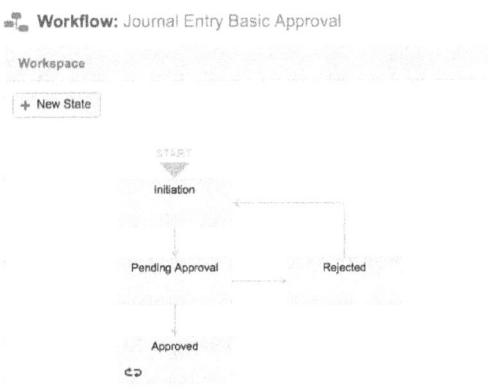

This basic workflow provides a great opportunity to take apart an approval workflow to see how workflows operate in NetSuite. Workflows aren't a primary focus of this book, but they can be key when building mitigating controls in NetSuite.

Audit Trail

Another important tool for mitigating risk in NetSuite is the built-in Audit Trail feature. For most financial transactions in NetSuite, an audit trail is established using system notes. These audit trails are searchable and can be used in alerts. Even better, this feature doesn't have to be turned on, and it's not editable by any user, even privileged users.

Changes to roles, customizations released into the system, transactions, and other common changes can all be tracked via system notes, with a few exceptions. Saved search alerts can be used to identify items outside of ordinary processing.

For example, a saved search alert could be used to notify someone about transactions created by users who normally wouldn't create specific transaction types. Specifically, a company may want to identify any Purchase Orders created by accounts payable users because they are part of the procure-to-pay process and shouldn't normally create POs.

Monitoring POs created by accounts payable could allow management to detect questionable transactions, especially if the user is involved in another part of the process. Monitoring changes to credit levels, terms, and addresses are other examples of changes that can be monitored through saved searches.

There may be some exceptions, but NetSuite works to reduce these exceptions with each new version. Search NetSuite Help for Audit Trail to identify current exceptions. For example, with version 2017.2, changes to workflows now log the following to system notes: that a change was made and the workflow revision number. More detailed information about a given change is still available in the history subtab on the workflow definition page.

To review a simple audit trail:
1. Select **Lists > Relationships > Customers** to get a list of customers.
2. Select **Audit Trail** in the upper right of the window.

3. On the **Audit Trail** page, set the criteria for the search. For our simple example, we'll skip the criteria. System notes can be searched by:

- The user ID of the person who made change.
- The date and time the change was made.
- The type of change (for example, whether the field was set for the first time or updated from a previous value).
- The field changed.
- The value before the change.
- The value after the change.
- The context for the change. For more information on context, search *Understanding the Context for Changes* in Help.

4. Click **Submit**.

The resulting audit trail shows the record information, who made the change, the date and time of the change, plus the old value and the new value.

Saved Searches

Being able to search audit records when the item is known is helpful, but usually it's not enough. Broader searches of system notes for audit trail information are available via NetSuite's **Saved Search** feature. This is a key feature for auditing and mitigating risks. To create a saved search of system notes:

1. Select **Reports > New Search**.
2. Scroll down and select **System Note.**
3. On the **System Note Search** page, set the criteria for the search. This is just like the audit trail search we looked at above.
4. For our simple example, move down to **Date**. Leave the setting at **within**. In the box next to **within** use the dropdown to pick **Next Month**.

As a reminder, system notes can be searched by:

- The user ID of the person who made change.
- The date and time the change was made.
- The type of change (for example, whether the field was set for the first time or updated from a previous value).
- The field changed.
- The value before the change.
- The value after the change.
- The context for the change. For more information on context, search *Understanding the Context for Changes* in Help.

5. Click **Submit**.

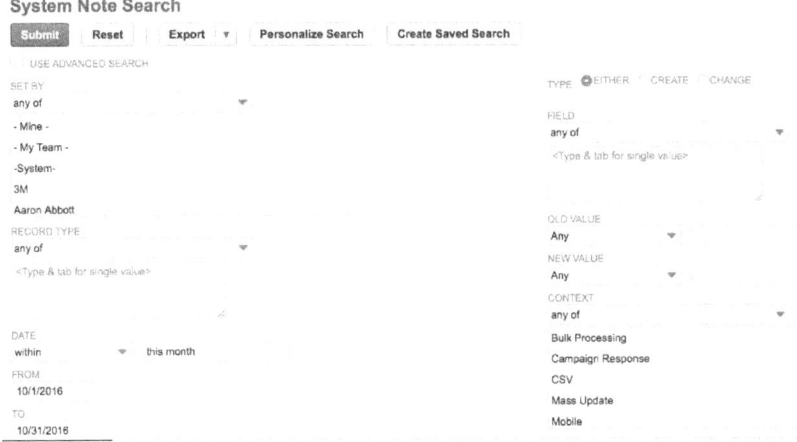

The resulting audit trail shows the record information, who made the change, the date and time of the change, plus the old value and the new value.

6. To save this search to use later, click the button marked **Save This Search**.

7. Give the search a title in **Search Title**. For this example, use *Audit Trail System Notes Test.*

8. Use the subtabs to set any additional details for the report.

9. Click **Save**.

Results can also be exported to Excel or PDF using the related icons at the upper left.

Emailing Saved Searches

Saved searches can function as review tool to mitigate risk. As a quick example, in a small A/P department, it may be difficult to properly segregate vendor creation and invoice entry. We've seen that workflows can be an option to require approval when new vendors are created. We've mentioned that another option would be to have a user not involved in the process perform a review of vendor creation and changes via a saved search. This user would then match the changes to documents substantiating the change, like an invoice or a vendor change notice.

A process like this works much better if the report can be delivered automatically on a schedule. NetSuite's Saved Search feature includes the ability to email a report. Let's look at how to do that.

1. Navigate to **Reports > Saved Searches > All Saved Searches**.
2. Scroll down to find the **Audit Trail System Notes Test** saved search that we created earlier and click edit.
3. Select the **Email** subtab.
4. Check the box marked **Send Emails According to Schedule**.
5. Check the box marked **Summarize Scheduled Emails**. This provides a single report with all the saved search information. Unchecking this box makes NetSuite send one email per record. In a review scenario, people are easily overwhelmed with the interruptions of one email per record so we'll keep the Summarize box checked.
6. Check the box **Send If No Results**. This sends an email even if there aren't new records to review. It lets the reviewer know that the report is working; there just aren't any new records.

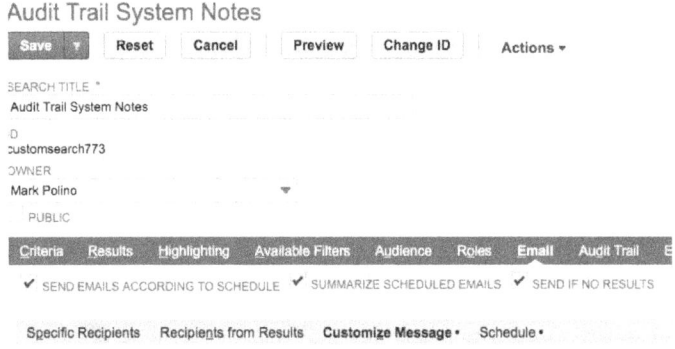

7. In the subtabs below email, pick **Specific Recipients** to send the search to specific reviewers. Optionally, recipients from results could be used to send an email to users with records in the search.

8. Select the **Customize Message** subtab to customize the sender, subject, and email body.

9. Select the **Schedule** tab to schedule the email.

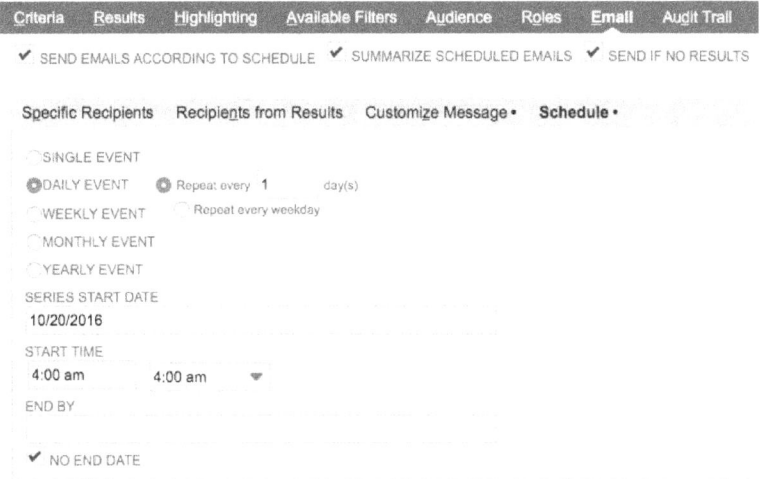

10. Click **Save** to save the email settings.

Problems with reviews include validating that they are being completed and completed within the specified time frame. Usually a signature and date are used as evidence of timely completion. NetSuite doesn't provide electronic sign-off for reviews. Fastpath's Assure tool offers electronic delivery and sign-off for access reviews and audit trail information.

Saved Search Email Alerts

Alerts can provide information when a selected event happens instead of on a fixed schedule. Recipients and subscribers receive email messages whenever search results are added to the saved search, and in some cases, when the results are updated. By default, email alerts are triggered whenever a newly added record matches criteria defined in the saved search.

There is also a **Send on Update** option to trigger alerts whenever an existing record is updated to match criteria defined in the saved search. Update alerts optionally can include information about recent changes. Update alerts can also be filtered so they will only be sent when certain fields change or when certain values occur.

If a saved search is made inactive, any email alert related to that saved search will not be triggered. The email alert will still exist in the system, but it will not trigger, and no email will be sent.

Email alerts are not available for all types of saved searches. For a list of these record types, search *Types of Saved Searches Available for Alerts* in NetSuite Help. Email alerts are also not available for searches with summarized results. For more information, search *Summary Types for Search Results* in Help.

A separate alert email message is sent to each recipient for every record add and, if applicable, update. If a group defined as an alert recipient has an email address, the alert is sent to that address; otherwise, alert emails are sent to individual addresses of group members.

Each alert message usually includes one result row because the search is filtered by the triggered record. Alerts can include multi-row results for searches that may return multiple rows for each triggering record, such as transaction searches, but given the nature of alerts, this generally doesn't deliver a good result.

 If a saved search with an email alert defined is included in a bundle, note that in target accounts where the bundle is installed, the email alert is not sent unless the **Enable Email Alerts for WS and CSV Imports** preference is enabled, at **Setup > Company > Email > Email Preferences.**

There are a lot of caveats around setting up alerts. Let's look at what's required to set up an alert.

1. Validate that the type of saved search being used allows alerts. Currently the list includes:
   - Campaign
   - Case
   - Contact
   - Customer
   - Employee
   - Event
   - Issue
   - Item

o   Opportunity

o   Partner

o   Phone Call

o   Project (if Project Management is enabled)

o   Solution

o   Task

o   Transaction

o   Vendor

For our example, I grabbed a saved search labeled **Assembly Items**, but any saved searches that fit the list will do.

1. **Navigate to Reports > Saved Searches > All Saved Searches**.

2. Scroll down to find a saved search and click **Edit.**

3. Select the **Email** subtab.

4. Check the box marked **Send Email Alerts When Records Are Created/Updated.** If this option is not available, it means alerts are not available for this type of saved search.

5. To allow users other than the selected recipients to receive this search's alerts, enable the **Public** and **Allow Users to Subscribe** options.

    o   Check the **Public** box under the **Owner** field on the **Saved Items Search** page.

    o   On the **Specific Recipients** subtab, below the **Email** subtab, check the **Allow Users to Subscribe** option.

6. To specify recipients by user name and/or group name, click the **Specific Recipients** subtab.

    o   To allow these recipients to receive alerts for updates as well as adds, select the **Send on Update** option.

- o If the **Send on Update** option is enabled, select
  Show Recent Changes to include information
  about changes.
- o Click **Add**.

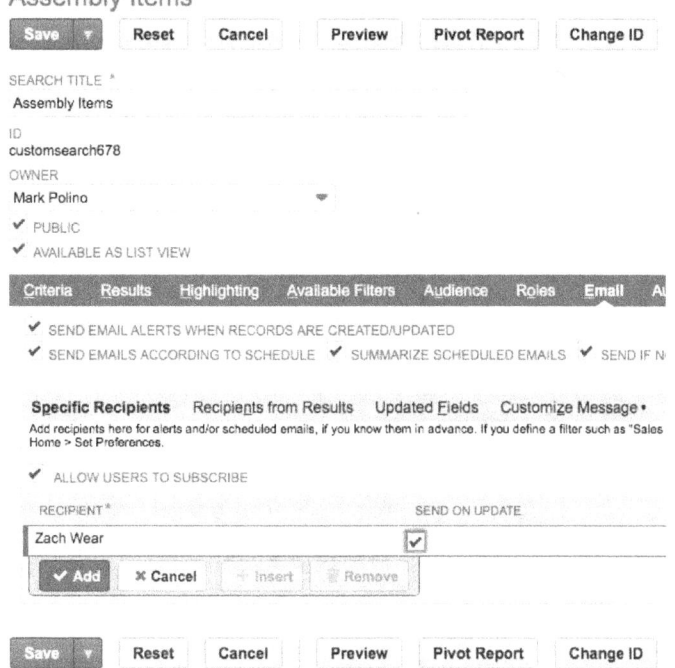

 Fastpath Audit Trail provides additional
features beyond NetSuite's built-in Audit
Trail. Fastpath Audit Trail provides
improved reporting options for system
notes and its snapshot technology delivers
options to audit items not available with
NetSuite's Audit Trail.

109

Analytics Audit Trail

NetSuite's Saved Search feature is extremely useful for digging into audit trail data, but what if someone changes and re-saves a search? A user could get very different results from what they expect. Also, what happens if a user deletes a commonly used saved search? How would someone know? That's where **Analytics Audit Trail** is useful. Analytics Audit Trail searches and displays audit trail data covering changes to all saved searches, custom reports, report schedules, and financial report layouts. For example, Analytics Audit Trail can be used determine whether a saved search has been deleted. In our example, we'll search for the schedule change we made earlier to a saved search.

To run an Analytics Audit Trail search:
1. Go to **Reports > New Search**.
2. Click **Analytics Audit Trail**.
3. Use the **Record Type** list to specify the record types to be included in the search. Select **Search** to find the schedule changes we made earlier to a saved search.

The following combinations of record types are available:
- **Financial Layout** – Select this option to find the changes made to financial report layouts.
- **Report** – Select this option to find the changes made to saved custom reports.
- **Report Schedule** – Select this option to find the changes made to report schedules.
- **Search** – Select this option to find the changes made to saved searches.

For specific changes, use the **Record Action field**. For changes related to a specific search or report, specify its name in the **Record** field. For our example, leave these blank.

4. To define the search further, use the following fields:
    o **Date** – For changes during a specific period, enter the period.
    o **From/To** – Enter the start and end dates for the period.
    o **Component Name** – For changes to a specific search or report component, enter the name of the component.
    o **Component Type** – For changes to search or report components of a specific type, enter this type.
    a. **Component Action** – For a specific action that resulted in changes, enter this action.
    b. The **Old Value** and **New Value** fields can be used to look for specific values before or after the change.
5. For our example, in **Component Type** select **Any Of** and highlight **Schedule**

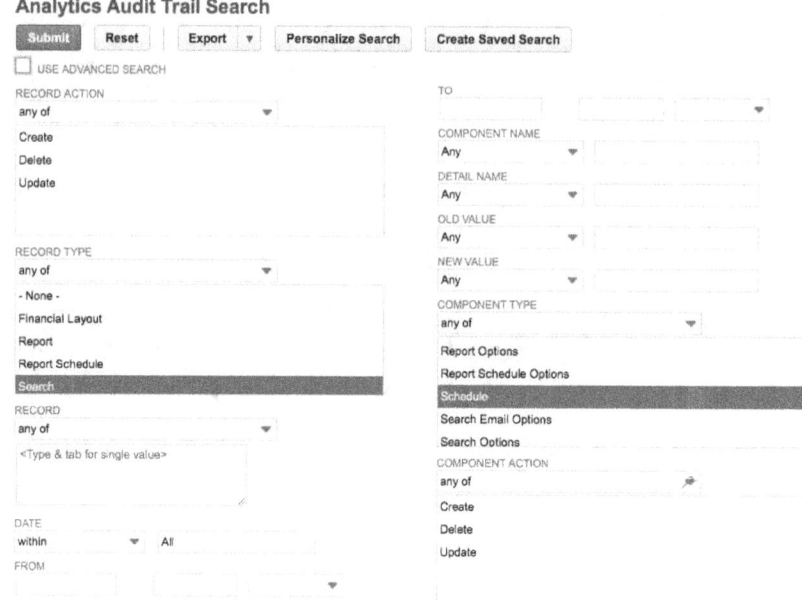

6. Click **Submit** to see the changes, or **Create Saved Search** to create a saved search based on the criteria.

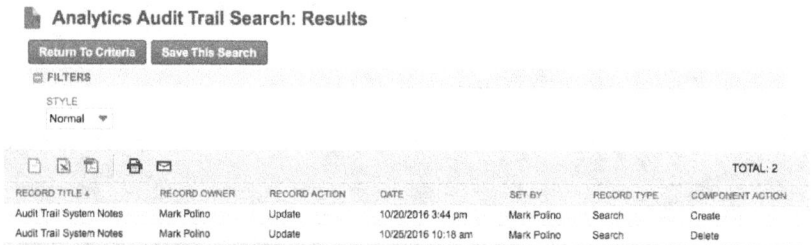

Analytics Audit Trail Searches provide a great way to review changes to searches and reports.

GL Audit Numbering

A fairly common audit request is a list of GL transactions, preferably without number gaps that would indicate missing transactions. This also helps companies meet international auditing requirements. NetSuite's

GL Audit Numbering feature applies gapless numbering sequences to all GL posting transactions. When this feature is enabled, GL Audit Numbering is listed as a required task when closing accounting periods. Running GL Audit Numbering at period end applies numbers to transactions in closed periods for the purposes of GL auditing.

From this task on the period close checklist, two types of numbering sequences are available: Permanent and Repeatable. With a Permanent GL audit numbering sequence, the number assigned to a GL impacting transaction cannot be changed. For a Repeatable GL audit numbering sequence, the numbering sequence on GL impacting transactions can be rerun as often as required.

Before this feature can be used, it needs to be enabled. To enable GL Audit Numbering:

1. Go to **Setup > Company > Enable Features**.
2. Select the **Accounting** tab.
3. Check the box next to **GL Audit Numbering** and click **Save.**

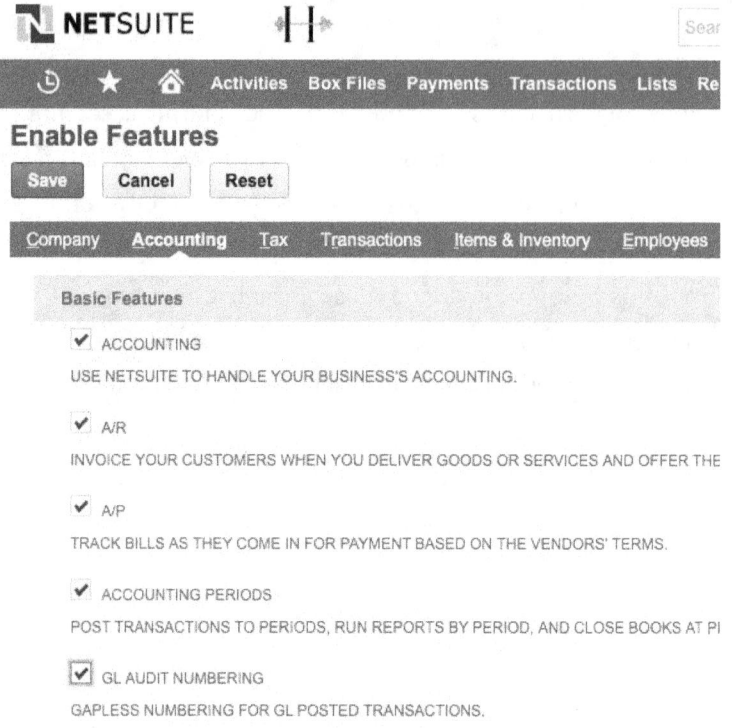

Next, choose the frequency of GL Audit Numbering:

4. Go to **Setup > Accounting > Preferences > Accounting Preferences.**

5. On the **General** subtab under **General Ledger**, find the field labeled **GL Audit Numbering Method**. Use the dropdown to select **Base Accounting Period, Quarter**, or **Year** to indicate the period end that will make the GL Audit Numbering task available as part of a period close.

6. Click **Save.**

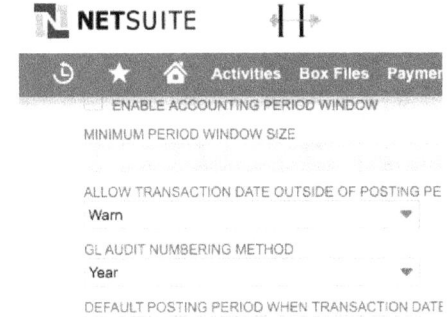

Finally, set the reporting and search preferences.

7. Go to **Home** > **Set Preferences**.

8. Select the **Analytics** subtab.

9. In the **Report by Period** list, select **Financials Only** or **All Reports** and hit **Save**. Selecting Financials Only filters the GL Audit Numbering Report by accounting period.

 Numbering G/L transactions is controlled by the **Manage Accounting Periods** permission. GL Audit Numbering is independent of other auto generated numbering set up at **Setup > Company > Setup Tasks > Auto-Generated Numbers**.

In the last month of a period, GL Audit Numbering can be set up for that period to have NetSuite generate and assign a number sequence. For example, if Quarterly was selected in the GL Audit Numbering Method we set earlier, this process can be done in the last month of the quarter.

 For NetSuite OneWorld, sequences can be created for each subsidiary. If the Multi-Book Accounting feature is used, book-specific GL numbering sequences can be created.

 The same sequence of numbers assigned to a period's transactions could be assigned to the transactions in another period if the sequence is defined in the same way. To avoid this, ensure that the sequences assigned to each period are unique, by using a prefix for example.

To set up a GL Audit Numbering sequence:

1. Using the **Period Close Checklist** at **Setup > Accounting > Manage Accounting Periods,** complete the items that precede the GL Audit Numbering task.

2. Click the **Go To Task** icon (white, right-facing arrow in a green circle) next to **GL Audit Numbering**.

3. Click the **GL Audit Numbering** button.

4. On the **GL Audit Numbering Setup** page, enter a name for the sequence.

   - For Multi-Book Accounting, select the accounting book to set the numbering sequence for.

   - For OneWorld, select the subsidiary to include in the sequence. The CTRL key can be used to select multiple subsidiaries.

5. Enter a prefix and/or suffix to apply around the numbers.

6. Enter the maximum number of digits permitted for each number.

7. Enter the first number to assign in this sequence.

8. Use the **Order By** column to choose how to order the transactions for numbering.

9. Click **Save.**

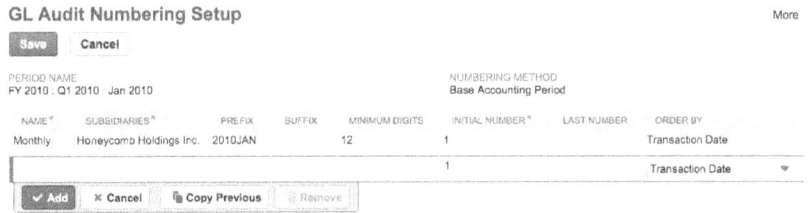

 For G/L numbering sequences created by base
accounting periods, the name, prefix, and
suffix from the previous period are
automatically set for the next period's
sequence. The first number in the sequence
is set to one higher than the last number of the
previous period's sequence, providing consistency
in numbering between periods.

The next step is to run the GL number sequences. During period close, GL numbering can be run as often as needed to address gaps in numbering that might occur due to GL adjustments. The GL Audit Numbering task is only available in the last month of the period.

To run GL numbering sequences:

1. Return to the **GL Audit Numbering** page via the **Period Close Checklist**.
2. Check the box next to the sequence to run.
3. Click **Run**.
4. Click **Validate** to verify that the box next to each sequence is gapless.

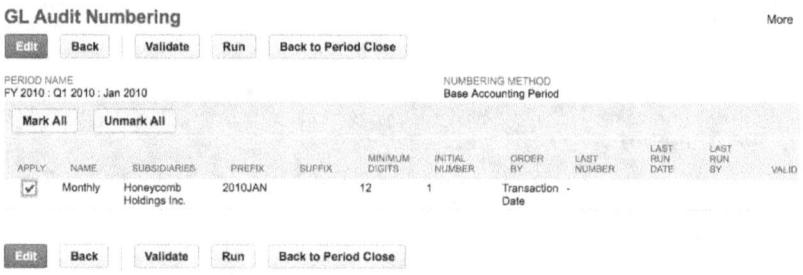

5. Click **Edit** or **Back** to return to the GL Audit Numbering Setup page.

6. Click **Back to Period Close** to return to the Period Close Checklist.

When finished, remember to mark the task complete as part of the period close process.

The **GL Audit Numbering** page provides information specific to the date and time the sequence was run, sequence name, numbers assigned, percent complete, status, date range, and number of records found. The **GL Audit Numbering History** page provides information specific to the base accounting period including whether it is closed.

Using GL Impact Locking

GL Impact Locking is a hidden option. For companies or subsidiaries located in a country where the GL impact of a transaction must be locked to the GL and must not be changed, companies can request that GL Impact Locking be enabled.

To request that GL Impact Locking be enabled in an account, enter a case record and provide the sCompID of the production or sandbox account where the option should be enabled. When the request is approved, NetSuite will manually enable GL Impact Locking.

When GL Impact Locking is enabled, any change to a GL numbered impacting transaction automatically generates a GL Impact Adjustment Copy and a GL Impact Adjustment Reversal transaction. These transactions display on the GL Impact subtab on the original GL impacted transaction. This subtab provides the history of GL Impact Copy and GL Impact Adjustment transactions. From each line, a link is provided to access the transaction details.

GL Impact Locking can be enabled for companies in accounts that are not OneWorld and for subsidiaries in accounts that are OneWorld.

More details on GL Impact Locking are available by searching for *GL Impact Locking* in NetSuite Help.

Use Deletion Reason

In some countries, there is a legal requirement to provide a reason why a transaction was deleted. In other cases, companies simply want to track a reason for deletion. Often auditors won't rely on the reason for the deletion, but it can be useful reminding users why a transaction was removed. This can be helpful for explaining the transaction or identifying supporting documents.

To support this, NetSuite offers the **Use Deletion Reason** feature. To activate Use Deletion Reason:

1. Go to **Setup > Company > Enable Features**.

2. Under **ERP General**, check the box marked **Use Deletion Reason.**

3. Click **Save**.

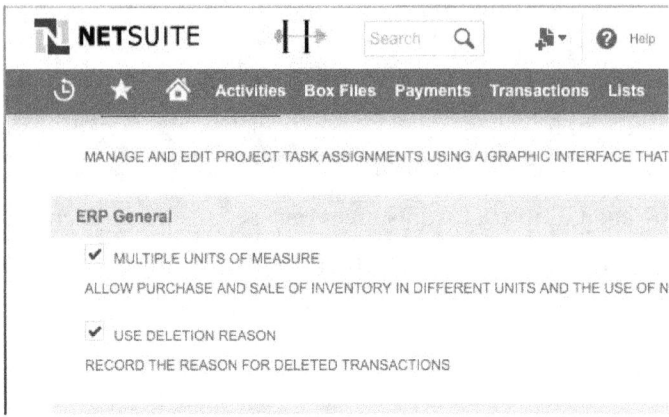

To see the transaction types affected by this feature:

1. Navigate to **Setup > Company > Auto-Generated Numbers**.

2. Select the **Document Numbers** subtab to see the affected transaction types.

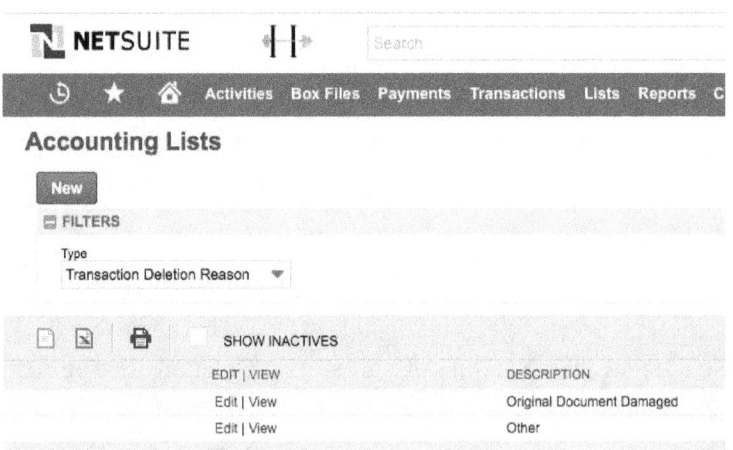

With this feature is enabled, users must provide a reason for deleting a transaction record. The **Transaction Numbering Audit Log** provides a list of the deleted transactions, the deletion reason, their transaction number, the date on which the transaction was deleted and by whom.

The Use Deletion Reason feature includes two standard deletion reasons: **Original Document Damaged** and **Other**. These two deletion reasons are available throughout the NetSuite account.

If users choose the standard deletion reason **Original Document Damaged,** writing a memo is optional. If users choose the standard deletion reason **Other,** a memo is required.

Users with the Administrator role or access to Accounting Lists can create and modify deletion reasons. To create, modify, inactivate, and choose display languages for a unique deletion reason:

1. Go to **Setup > Accounting > Accounting Lists**.
2. Filter the list to show **Transaction Deletion Reason**.
3. Click **New** to set up a new deletion reason.
4. Enter the reason and click **Save.**

Transaction deletion reasons are case sensitive, must be unique to avoid duplication, and cannot exceed 30 characters.

If the **Transaction Deletion Reason** feature is later disabled, deleted transactions will no longer require a reason. The Transaction Numbering Audit Log will retain the reason for previously deleted transactions.

Journal Entry Approval

NetSuite offers a few options for approval of journal entries. For most organizations, a workflow like the Journal Entry Basic Approval workflow shown earlier in this chapter is the preferred option, but there are other choices. The original option is the **Require Approvals on Journal Entries** feature and the newest option is **SuiteApprovals for Journal Entry**.

The options can't be used together. For example, If **Journal Entries** is checked in **Setup > Accounting > Accounting Preferences** under the **Approval Routing** subtab, then a workflow approval is active and the **Require Approvals on Journals Entries** check box will be unavailable.

To activate the **Require Approvals on Journals Entries** feature:

1. Select **Setup > Accounting > Accounting Preferences**.

2. In the **General** section, check the box marked **Require Approvals on Journal Entries**.

3. Click **Save**.

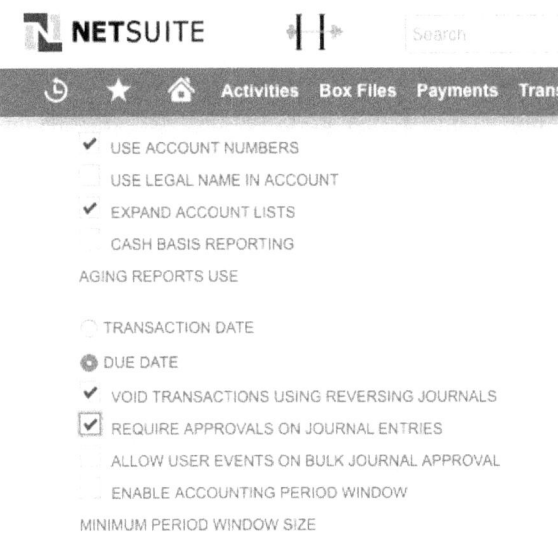

When either preference is enabled, users with Journal Approval permission must approve a journal entry before the entry posts to the general ledger.

 Users with Journal Approval permission can approve their own journal entries when entering them.

After approval, NetSuite posts journal entries to the general ledger. A journal entry is posted in a period to which the journal entry approver has access. Until a journal entry is approved, NetSuite tentatively displays the posting period based on the transaction date, or, if this period is locked/closed, the first open period.

To approve a journal entry using either option:
1. Go to **Transactions > Financial > Approve Journal Entries**.
2. Check the box in the **Approve** column next to the journal entries to approve. If a custom workflow is used, two lists

appear at the top of the page. The **Action** list enables approval or rejection. The **View** list is used to filter journal entries by their status. Other buttons may also appear depending on the workflow specifics.

3. Click **Save**.

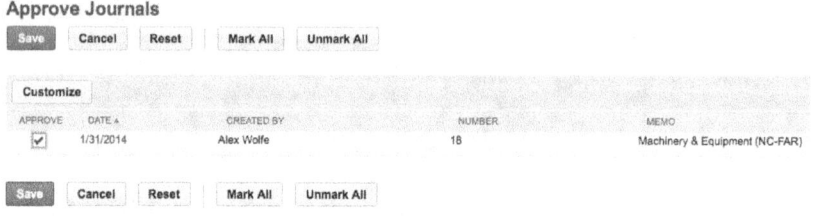

SuiteApprovals for Journal Entry is a new feature in 2017.2. It is designed to provide standard capabilities for managing journal entry approval. SuiteApprovals customizable properties, help ensure that only authorized individuals can edit, approve, reject, and resubmit journal entries for approval. Administrators can create approval rules, each consisting of a set of criteria and approval hierarchy, to manage the validation and approval routing of journal entries. Conceptually this is the same as creating a workflow, but the setup is designed specifically around journal entry approval and it is isolated from other workflow designers.

To install SuiteApprovals for Journal Entry, go to Customization > SuiteBundler > Search & Install Bundles.

Use the following information to search for the SuiteApp:

Bundle Name: **SuiteApprovals**
Bundle ID: **203059**

The SuiteApprovals for Journal Entry SuiteApp is a managed bundle and is automatically updated for issue fixes and enhancements.

By default, the Administrators and Full Accessfollowing roles are given full access to the SuiteApprovals for Journal Entry SuiteApp.

Other roles need additional permissions to use the SuiteApp. The table below outlines the permissions required for using SuiteApprovals for Journal Entry. For information about customizing roles, see Customizing or Creating NetSuite Roles.

Permission	Level
To allow a custom role to set up approval rules:	
Approval Rule record	Full
Approval Matrix record	Full
To allow a custom role to set up approval information and delegation:	
Lists > Employees	Edit
To allow a custom role to set up roles, departments, or groups:	
Setup > Bulk Manage Roles	Full
Lists > Departments	Full
Lists > CRM Groups	Full
To allow a custom role to set up Department Approvers:	
Department Approver record	Full
Lists > Custom Record Entries	Full

Permission	Level
Lists > Departments	Full
Lists > Subsidiaries	Full
Lists > Employees	Full

After customizing a role to access SuiteApprovals lists and records, an administrator must also add this new role to the corresponding script deployment.

NetSuite provides full documentation for installing, setting up, and using SuiteApprovals for Journal Entry by searching the help topic SuiteApprovals for Journal Entry. SuiteApprovals for Journal Entry can provide a comprehensive approval solution, like workflows, with prebuilt options and isolated from other workflows and workflow creators.

Absolute Session Timeouts

The Open Web Application Security Project (OWASP) provides a guideline that all sessions should implement an absolute timeout, regardless of session activity. The absolute session timeout limits the amount of time possible for a potential attacker to use a hijacked session to impersonate a user.

This timeout defines the maximum amount of time a session can be active. The session is closed and invalidated upon the defined absolute period, because the given session was initially created by the web application. After the session is invalidated, the user must authenticate (log in) again in the web application and establish a new session.

To provide enhanced login security and comply with the guideline, NetSuite 2017.2 includes these enhancements:

- Account administrators can now customize the idle session timeout in minutes on the General Preferences page.
- Users now see a 60 second countdown warning when their session is about to expire and can choose to keep the session active by clicking a button in this warning.
- If a user has multiple browser tabs open, session management will now be synced across these tabs. Tabs will be locked on logout and unlocked on login.
- When a user changes role, any tabs left open from the previous session will be shown as inactive and locked if the user switches back to that same role.
- Users logged in with a role that has access to view unencrypted credit card data will be subject to an idle session timeout of 15 minutes in accordance with section 8.1.8 of PCI DSS.
- In previous versions of NetSuite, a 24-hour absolute session timeout was added. This has been reduced to 12 hours in accordance with NIST Digital Identity Guidelines for Authentication and Lifecycle Management.

Other Controls

NetSuite includes a number of other built-in controls that are an important, if often overlooked, portion of the control fabric. Some of these are active out of the box and some require minimal configuration. We won't go into detail on these items, and this isn't an exhaustive list, but they are important items to note.

The following internal controls do not require any set up after a firm's NetSuite account is operational.[8]

Accounts Receivable
- Outstanding invoices are aged and added to an A/R aging report in real time.

Financial Close
- General ledger accounts automatically roll up into financial statement line items.
- The financial statement consolidation process is performed on a real-time basis.
- The general ledger is automatically configured to include all accounts with balances.
- All transactions automatically roll up into the general ledger in real time.
- Transactions cannot be posted to closed periods in NetSuite.
- Out of balance transactions are automatically rejected.
- Transactions referencing a closed period are automatically rejected.
- Transactions containing an invalid or inactive GL segment, for example, account or cost center, are automatically rejected.
- CTA (Cumulative Translation Adjustments) are automatically calculated in NetSuite.
- FX (currency translation) related adjustments are automatically calculated in NetSuite.
- Access to open and close the GL accounting period in NetSuite is restricted to selected users.

---

[8] NetSuite, NetSuite Help "Internal Controls in NetSuite" NetSuite.com (November 2016)

- Allocation weight is dynamically calculated when an allocation journal is generated, based on the current statistical account balance.
- Elimination journal entries are automatically generated based on intercompany transactions.
- Password strength for access to NetSuite accounts is required to comply with password policy.
- Calculation is automatic for a reversing journal entry that voids checks and transactions on days or periods different from the original transaction date.
- Journal entries require approval in line with Journal Entry Approval Policy prior to posting to the general ledger.
- Transactions posted outside of a posting period can be prevented or can initiate a warning.
- Limitations can be set on the individuals who can impact the account listed on an item record.
- A gapless numbering sequence is applied to all GL posting transactions.

Financial Reporting
- Financial statements are automatically generated for each separate entity in NetSuite.
- Financial reports for each entity are automatically prepared in their local currency and are converted in real time into headquarters currency for consolidation purposes.

Fixed Assets
- NetSuite automatically calculates depreciation expense.
- The Fixed Asset Module automatically calculates and posts the depreciation expense to the asset record and to the related journal entries to the general ledger.

Inventory

- NetSuite values inventory at standard cost.
- Inventory transactions created and/or edited in closed periods can be disallowed.

IT General Controls

- A minimum password length is required to comply with password policy.
- Users are required to update their passwords with a regular frequency.
- System notes are captured on the creation of all records and are not editable by users.
- System notes are captured on the edit of all records and are not editable by users.
- System notes are captured on the import and export of all custom fields.

Order to Cash

- Items purchased in a sales order for a customer are automatically reflected in the invoice and are automatically sent to the customer by email when the **Save & Email** button on the Next Bill tab is clicked. The order status of the sales order is automatically changed to Partially Fulfilled (several invoices or installment) or Billed (single invoice).
- For orders on an installment basis, the billing schedule in the body of a sales order for a customer is automatically populated in NetSuite and can be viewed on the History tab of the customer record. This tab indicates scheduled billing dates and amounts for each date.
- Upon invoicing, NetSuite automatically generates an entry.
- NetSuite prevents creation of a customer with a blank credit limit.
- NetSuite creates invoices only after an order has been shipped.

- NetSuite restricts changes made to item quantity, pricing, and shipping income per sales order during the invoicing process.
- NetSuite books an entry to debit accounts receivable and to credit Revenue upon invoice creation.
- NetSuite places an order on hold when the customer exceeds the assigned credit limit. There is a workflow trigger, in which an increase in the credit limit, if applicable, is generated and approved by the CFO.
- When a customer exceeds their credit limit, NetSuite can enforce an automatic hold or simply initiate a warning message.
- Orders entered into NetSuite, but not yet billed, can be included in customer credit limit calculations.
- Standard grace periods for overdue invoices prior to placing a customer on hold can be set up in line with the customer credit policy.
- Edits to previously approved sales orders are disallowed.
- NetSuite prohibits users from making any changes to a revenue recognition schedule for a transaction after the A/R period has been closed.

Procure to Pay
- Records and transactions can optionally be limited by the department of the individual entering or editing them.
- Records and transactions can optionally be limited by the class of the individual entering or editing them.
- Records and transactions can optionally be limited by the location of the individual entering or editing them.

Revenue
- NetSuite does not allow revenue recognition greater than 100% of the total amount of the project.

Time Entry

- Time entry requires supervisor approval.
- There is a maximum number of hours an employee can enter for a given week in line with the Human Capital Management (HCM) policy.
- There is a maximum number of hours an employee can enter for a given day in line with the HCM policy.
- There is a minimum number of hours an employee can enter for a given day in line with the HCM policy.

The following controls require some basic setup in the NetSuite UI[9]:

Accounts Receivable

- Open receivables identified by user-defined conditions, such as large invoices or exceeding the credit limit, are automatically identified and routed for review.

Financial Close

- The amount of expense to be amortized per month is automatically spread based on the amortization schedule prepared by A/P.
- NetSuite automatically allocates the expenses to different departments based on the allocation percentages.
- Access to open and close the sub-ledgers (A/P, A/R, and Payroll) and the general ledger is restricted to approved roles.
- Elimination journal entries are automatically generated based on intercompany drop-ship workflow transactions.
- Intercompany accounts are automatically reconciled.

Commissions

---

[9] NetSuite, NetSuite Help "Internal Controls in NetSuite" NetSuite.com (November 2016)

- Monthly, NetSuite automatically calculates eligible commission amounts based on the plan type linked to the participant (employee or partner).
- After a commission is approved, it is automatically posted to A/P and to the general ledger, and is auto-populated for the payroll run.
- Commissions are calculated and processed in line with standard compensation agreements.

Fixed Assets

- Edit access to the Fixed Asset Module (FAM) is restricted to users with approved roles only.
- NetSuite FAM is configured to calculate monthly depreciation based on the asset's cost, depreciation method, and useful life.

Human Resources and Payroll

- Edit access to the Payroll folder, which contains the Payroll Worksheet, is restricted to users with approved roles.
- NetSuite auto-populates employee hours and expenses after appropriate approvals are obtained in the system.
- Once a payroll is committed, the related payroll taxes, benefits, bonuses, and commission expenses are automatically calculated and posted to the general ledger.

IT General Controls

- NetSuite compares contact and customer records and provides notifications of possible duplicate records.
- Employee access can be restricted based upon IP address.

Order to Cash

- A general ledger journal entry is automatically created when an authorized credit memo is created and approved.
- A journal entry is automatically generated when a batch payment posting is created and approved.

- After all payments from a bank batch are applied, a deposit activity is performed in NetSuite and the related journal entry is automatically generated.
- When payment from the bank for a single activity is applied, a deposit activity is performed in NetSuite, and the related journal entry to accounts receivable is automatically generated.
- Unbilled approved T&M hours are automatically populated in NetSuite for invoicing.
  NetSuite only allows fulfillment and shipment of inventory if the following conditions are met:
  o Sales order is in Pending Fulfillment or Partially Fulfilled status and is not on hold for any reason.
  o Part numbers of items being fulfilled match part numbers on the Sales order and the quantity being fulfilled does not exceed the quantity on the sales order.
  o For serialized inventory items, such as switches, each fulfilled serial number matches a serial number that exists in finished goods inventory.
- Shipping amounts are automatically calculated and applied to transactions based on rules.
- A 1099 or W2 is required prior to vendor approval.

Procure to Pay
- NetSuite automatically routes a PO for approval based on the approval policy set. Only POs that have been properly approved can be processed for invoicing.
- Spending thresholds on POs are built into a workflow as required by governance.
- Spending thresholds on non-PO spending are built into a workflow as required by governance.

- Use of vendors in purchase orders is restricted to pre-approved vendors.
- Updates to vendor information route automatically for review to designated approvers.
- Non-inventory purchase requests are automatically routed for approval request to the relevant reviewer/approver.
- Inventory purchase requests are automatically routed for approval request to the relevant reviewer/approver.
- A three-way match is automatically performed for POs that have lines mapped to item receivable general ledger accounts. The control is configured at the item level. If any item quantity or price does not match, an error message is displayed, the invoice is not posted, and the invoice is placed in Pending Approval status in NetSuite.
- Expense reports are automatically routed to the employee's manager and, after approval by the manager, to A/P for review and approval. After approval by the employee manager and A/P, the expense report is marked for payment.
- Purchase requests are routed for approval based on set approval limits.
- Expense reports are routed for approval based on set approval limits.

Revenue

- The relative fair value allocation at the time of an invoice is applied. The allocations are based on the relative fair values for all line items in the invoice based on the Best Estimate Selling Price (BESP) data contained in NetSuite.
- On invoicing, NetSuite creates a service amortization schedule for all of the service line items on the invoice.

- NetSuite is set up to defer revenue and the related cost of sales per terms and conditions set out in the customer master file. These terms include: rights of return, acceptance, shipping terms, and others.

- NetSuite automatically recognizes and defers revenue based on the Revenue Recognition Policy. (Note: The Revenue Recognition Policy must be set up in NetSuite for each item.)

- NetSuite is configured to recognize revenue on a monthly straight-line basis, prorated daily basis for the first and last month, for subscription and support revenue based on the provisioned date, contract start and end dates, and revenue recognition schedule.

{6}

CUSTOMIZATIONS & SCRIPTS

- Access Review and Certification
- Role Management
- Emergency Management
- Monitoring

In Chapter 6, we take on customizations and scripts. Since customizations and scripts can make changes invisibly, and often with elevated security, they overlap with many of our security principles. Access to customizations are controlled by role management. Similarly, access to execute and create scripts are managed by roles.

Additionally, the process of creating customizations and scripts needs its own set of security and segregation of duties processes. Access review and certification applies to developers who write scripts and customizations. Emergency access management can be critical for fixing bugs, and all of this needs appropriate monitoring.

Principles

Application customization is an important control consideration. Customizations can fundamentally change the way that an application feature works, bypass security controls, or do any number of other things that could intentionally or unintentionally undermine security.

In many organizations, the term "customization" is associated with a formal customization project. Small changes like adding a field, making a field required, or using a script to change behavior aren't considered true customizations. When it comes to security, the term "customization" is broadly defined to include any change to the application that is not controlled via configuration.

In other words, if application behavior is changed by marking a checkbox or selecting an item from a dropdown list in the application, that is usually a configuration change. Adding fields or forms, using scripting to change the behavior of a form, and adding additional calculations are examples of simple customizations.

The key components to managing customizations and scripting are System Development Life Cycle (SDLC) and change management controls. These represent controls designed to provide a reasonable assurance that changes to production application systems are properly authorized, tested, approved, implemented, and documented. A strong, well-governed and documented SDLC and change management process, with proper segregation of duties enforced, will help ensure that only properly authorized and tested changes are promoted to production.

NetSuite doesn't provide access to allow users to make changes to source code, so this is where a review of NetSuite's SOC 1 report is important. Application changes like customizations, scripting, or workflows can be done at the application layer making it important for companies to develop their own SDLC and change management program.

There are some core principles and leading practices around SDLC and change management. These include:

- All change requests should be documented, ideally with a consistent form.
- Change requests should be properly approved.
- Developers should be prevented from promoting their own code to production.
- Developers should test their own code prior to promoting their code to the next step.
- Code changes should be documented and the change request should be updated at each step as it moves through the process.
- Appropriate segregation of duties should be in place to support development, testing, quality assurance, and release.
- The process should include emergency options to address.

Change Requests

All changes, regardless of where they start within the organization, should be documented on a standardized change request mechanism. The change mechanism should contain information like:

- Request Date
- Description of the requested change
- Business justification
- Assignment of the request
- Authorization for development work to begin
- Details of development, test, and user acceptance

- Approval for release
- Post-release sign-off

A submitted request should be routed to authorized individuals or groups for approval. The request can then be routed to other approvers as it moves through other steps in the process. Typical steps include:

- Initiation
- Development
- Testing/Quality Assurance
- User Acceptance Testing
- Production Release
- Production Verification

A system like this makes it easier to ensure that required fields are completed before tickets are closed, and that approvals are obtained before a change request moves to the next level. Attachments for things like test plans or summaries can be included as part of the process.

A leading practice for SDLC and change management is the use of a formal ticketing system and supporting process to provide point-in-time information on any given change identifying the environment the code change resides in, responsibility for the change, and the impact. To ensure this change request process is followed, companies need a standard procedure outlining the use of the change management system, the requirements for completeness, standards for accuracy in data, and a requirement for approvals as code moves from environment to environment. This process must be documented and available for review by the auditors.

Developers should test their code first, before it is ever passed on for testing and sign-off. Strong controls around testing need to be in place. These controls include a standard testing process that should be shared and consistent across functional departments. Testing documents should include information about what is being tested, inputs, expected outcomes, and documenting a "pass or fail" status to the test. These documents can also serve as audit evidence.

Tests should be clearly signed off on by the testers, including the date, and routed to the development or QA team as appropriate. No code should ever be moved forward in the development process without evidence of testing and sign-off, ideally with the test results themselves also documented and retained for audit.

Developers and testers should not be moving code between environments. This activity should be performed by a separate group to ensure adequate segregation of duties, but that group should not act without first receiving the proper documentation, including relevant code change request forms and testing documents.

Ideally, test results and sign-off information should be stored in the same repository as the change requests, and this repository should be designed in a way that it is easily searchable, well structured, and backed up such that the information is not lost if the repository data is damaged. Segregation of duties is as important a consideration in customizations as it is with financial transactions.

In environments in which personnel resources are scarce, and complete SoD is not possible, compensating controls should be created that minimize the chance of unapproved changes moving or being promoted to the next environment. For example, developers might promote the code of other developers to production, but not their own, and management could review and document all production code pushes.

Exceptions to change management processes will occasionally be necessary, so policies and procedures for handling such exceptions should exist, and specific occurrences of exceptions should be well documented. A common exception is an emergency code fix that bypasses normal code testing or shortcuts standard segregation of duties. All such exceptions should be documented, reviewed, and approved within a business reasonable period.

Many businesses are sensitive to disruptions around key financial windows, so it is recommended to avoid customization releases around end of month, quarter, or year.

Third-Party Applications

Policies, procedures, and controls should exist to govern and monitor the selection, installation, maintenance, and security of third-party applications installed within, or integrated with, a NetSuite account.

Selection processes should require the business owner and third-party provider (vendor) to clearly define:

- The nature and scope of features.
- Boundaries between the customer and partner application (who's responsible for what?).
- Where master data lives, i.e., which system is the source of truth.

- Service level agreements with respect to application performance and support.

In addition to the requirements of the business owner, selection criteria should also account for requirements from the legal, security, and compliance departments.

In this context, it is also important to understand partner maturity. Not all partners are equal and the same applies to their applications. The selection criteria should also consider topics such as:

- Reputation
- Years of service
- Fiscal responsibility and performance
- Size of install base
- Location and number of employees and contractors (developers, support, professional services)
- Use of subservice organizations and sub-contractors
- Availability of independent control environment certifications

Lastly, third-party vendor management policies, procedures, and controls should account for and manage the evolution of the contractual relationship, the companies, and the third-party application over time.

Application

SuiteBuilder

SuiteBuilder is a point-and-click interface that provides the ability to customize NetSuite to more closely align with individual business needs and processes. This allows non-developers to create custom fields, forms, record types, transactions, segments, and centers. These tools can be used to control how NetSuite users access information in an organization.

Fields

Custom fields can be added to entry forms or to transactions as part of the body or line items. Access to custom fields can be set at the record level as well as searches and reports based on the user's role, department, or subsidiary. If a user has different access levels between their role, department, or subsidiary, the highest access level is granted. The following access levels are available when creating custom fields:

- **Edit** – field is visible and can be changed
- **View** – field is visible but cannot be changed
- **Run** – field is visible in searches and reports but cannot be changed
- **None** – field is not visible and cannot be changed

Forms

Forms are used to view and enter data into NetSuite. A standard set of forms is provided with NetSuite out of the box and can be customized as needed to create new forms. Custom forms can be created for entities, transactions, and email or print versions of records.

It is possible to control which forms are available to users by making configuration changes during form creation or role setup. In form creation, users can set the **Form is Preferred** setting to make the given form the default when no other settings are in place. Companies can also use the **Roles** subtab to specify a form as preferred for select roles.

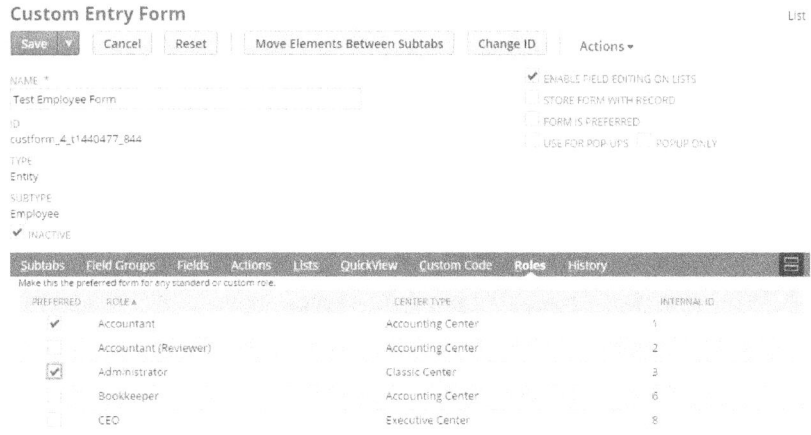

In role setup, it is possible to enable or disable custom forms by record type, set preferred forms, and restrict available forms. Setting a preferred form and turning on the **Restricted** setting will make the preferred form the only form available for that record type. In the example below, the Standard Assembly Build form is preferred for this role and is the only form available as indicated by the restricted setting.

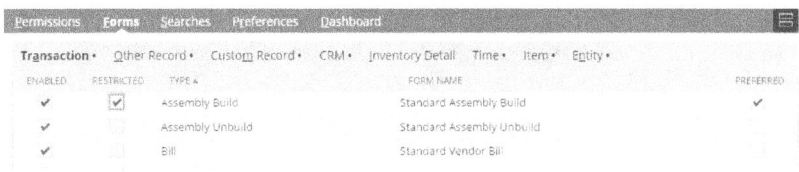

Record Types

Custom record types can be created to store data not collected by standard NetSuite records. When creating custom record types, there are several settings that can affect who has access to modify the record type definition as well as the individual instances of that record type.

Who can modify the record type definition?

When creating a custom record type, creators can specify the owner of that record type. By default, only the owner can modify that record type. Adding additional users with access to modify the record type is done via the **Managers** subtab. When added as a manager, that employee is automatically granted view access to that custom record.

Who can view or modify the record type instances?

There are several settings that determine which users are granted access to the instances of a custom record type.

- **Owners** – by default, owners have full access
- **Managers** – specified through the Managers subtab on the custom record, managers have view access by default
- **Access Type** – the Access Type field on the custom record has three different settings that determine how permissions are applied to instances of the custom record
  - **Require Custom Record Entries Permission (default)** – requires that the user has a role with the Custom Record Entries permission
  - **Use Permission List** – requires that user has a role defined on the Permissions subtab of the custom record
  - **No Permission Required** – all users may access
- **Role Restrictions** – restricts access to instances of the custom record based on the record's values for department, class, location, employee, and subsidiary fields. This requires the custom record to have list/record fields for department, class, location, employee, or subsidiary with the **Apply Role Restrictions** field enabled.
- **Field Access** – access to fields on a custom record can be limited using the same methodology available to custom fields.

Additional security settings:

- **Allow UI Access** – if disabled, access to instances of this custom record may only be accessed programmatically (enabled by default)
- **Allow Mobile Access** – determines if instances of this custom record are accessible through NetSuite mobile apps (disabled by default)
- **Enable System Notes** – determines if system notes are created for changes to instances of this record type (enabled by default)

Transactions

Custom transaction types are similar to custom records in that they can store data not collected by standard NetSuite records, with the added feature of recording an impact to the general ledger. Custom transaction types can have their own numbering scheme, permission model, and workflows. Permissions are defined on the **Permissions** subtab of the custom transaction type, which allows specifying the roles that have access along with the access levels. Alternatively, permissions for custom transactions may be granted by editing a specific role and adding the required permissions. By default, users with the Administrator or Full Access roles have full permissions.

Segments

The **Custom Segments** feature allows creation of custom classification fields like department, class, and location. These custom segments can then be added to specific record types and configured to display on the general ledger impact page and reports.

Who can manage custom segments?

By default, users with the Administrator or Full Access role can create and configure segments and segment values. It is possible to grant other users access by giving them the **Custom Segments** permission or manually adjusting permissions on the Custom Segment Permissions subtab.

 A user must have at least **View** access to the Custom Segments permission to manage custom segment definitions.

Who can use custom segments?

Permissions for using custom segments are defined on the custom segment definition using the **Permissions** subtab. This allows specifying which roles can use the segment on records or view the segment when using searches and reports. To use the segment, the user's role must have the **Record Access** permission. To view the segment in searches and reports, the user's role must have the **Search/Reporting Access** permission.

Auditing Changes to SuiteBuilder Components

Changes to most SuiteBuilder components can be monitored by searching against system notes in NetSuite.

1. Create a new saved search for the **System Note** record type

New Saved Search

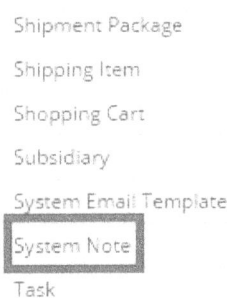

Shipment Package

Shipping Item

Shopping Cart

Subsidiary

System Email Template

System Note

Task

2. Add a new filter for the **Record Type** field. Optionally specify which component to review. In the example below, we are looking at custom fields.

3. Add the relevant fields under the **Results** tab. This typically includes the following:

    a. Record (individual record)

    b. Set By (who made the change)

    c. Date (when the change was made)

    d. Field (what field was changed on the record)

    e. Old Value (value before the change)

    f. New Value (value after the change)

The results of this search will provide insight into changes against SuiteBuilder components based on the record type specified under the search criteria. These changes should be able to tie back to existing change management processes.

 Changes to a component's access settings may not be visible in system note searches. Instead, these changes can be viewed by opening the specific component, clicking the Access subtab, then clicking the History subtab.

SuiteScript

As defined by NetSuite, SuiteScript is a JavaScript-based API that gives developers the ability to extend NetSuite beyond the capabilities provided through SuiteBuilder point-and-click customization. With SuiteScript (or 'scripts' as they are commonly referred to), developers can access NetSuite data programmatically to build complex custom business processes that are tailored to a specific organization's needs. Scripts are generally triggered via a specific user interaction, which can vary depending on the type of script.

Scripts in NetSuite consist of three components:

Source Files
JavaScript and other files that make up the business logic contained in the script. These files are stored in the NetSuite file cabinet. Typically, source files can be found in the SuiteScripts or SuiteBundles folders.

Script Record
Defines the type of script and links to the source files that contain the relevant business logic.

Script Deployment Record

Defines how the script is triggered, including the audience. The audience specifies for which users a given script will run in NetSuite and can be filtered based on role, department, subsidiary, group, or specific user. Without a deployment, scripts will not run.

There are many different types of scripts in NetSuite. The type of script will generally determine how the script is triggered but can also have an impact on the security context under which a given script will run. The script types are outlined below:

Client

Executed in a user's web browser and is typically used to modify how a user will interact with a record form.

- **Triggers:** action on a record form, such as the initial load of the form, entering or changing field values, modifying line items in a transaction, or saving a record
- **Security Context:** current user's role

User Event

Executed on the NetSuite server, user events are typically used to inject custom business logic into the record processing pipeline.

- **Triggers:** certain actions on records, such as loading, creating, deleting, editing, or copying
- **Security Context:** can be set to either the current user's role or a specific security role on the script deployment record for a user event script
- **Additional notes:** user event scripts can be set to run under the security context of the Administrator role (can only be set by administrators). In this case, it is critical to maintain strict

change management processes regarding the contents of the script.

Suitelet

Suitelets are executed on the NetSuite server and can be used to provide custom NetSuite pages or backend logic via an HTTP GET or POST request.

- **Triggers:** user navigation to a custom NetSuite page, HTTP GET or POST request
- **Security Context:** can be set to either the current user's role or a specific security role on the script deployment record for a suitelet script
- **Additional notes:** suitelet scripts can be set to run under the security context of the Administrator role (can only be set by administrators). In this case, it is critical to maintain strict change management processes regarding the contents of the script.

RESTlet

RESTlets are also executed on the NetSuite server and provide a custom web service endpoint for purposes of integration.

- **Triggers:** HTTP request
- **Security Context:** varies, each request requires security credentials
- **Additional notes:** request history is provided in NetSuite, associated to relevant integration record

Scheduled

Executed on the NetSuite server, scheduled scripts are ideal for long running tasks and batch jobs due to higher limit of usage governance.

- **Triggers:** on-demand or based on schedule
- **Security Context:** Administrator only

Portlet

Portlets are executed on the NetSuite server and provide custom dashboard capability.

- **Triggers:** user viewing a dashboard
- **Security Context:** can be set to either the current user's role or a specific security role on the script deployment record for a portlet script.
- **Additional notes:** portlet scripts can be set to run under the security context of the Administrator role (can only be set by administrators). In this case, it is critical to maintain strict change management processes regarding the contents of the script.

Mass Update

Mass update scripts allow custom mass update functionality that is not available through general mass updates.

- **Triggers:** user creates a custom mass update, filters to specific records, and manually starts the mass update
- **Security Context:** can be set to either the current user's role or a specific security role on the script deployment record for a mass update script
- **Additional notes:** mass update scripts can be set to run under the security context of the Administrator role (can only be set by administrators). In this case, it is critical to maintain strict change management processes regarding the contents of the script.

Workflow Action

Programmatic functions that can be added as an action to a workflow.

- **Triggers:** based on the workflow an action is added to.
- **Security Context:** can be set to either the current user's role or a specific security role on the script deployment record for a workflow action script
- **Additional notes:** workflow action scripts can be set to run under the security context of the Administrator role (can only be set by administrators). In this case, it is critical to maintain strict change management processes regarding the contents of the script.

Bundle Installation

Scripts that process data in a target account during bundle installation, update, or delete.

- **Triggers:** install, update, or delete of a SuiteBundle
- **Security Context:** Administrator

Auditing

Scripts are generally at the heart of NetSuite customization, with functionality ranging from simple data validation to advanced approval processes and completely custom business processes. Scripts can have a large impact on the business and the integrity of transactions being processed through NetSuite. With a wide-ranging set of functionality and the ability to run under elevated security contexts, it is important to regularly audit scripts and verify changes against an established change management process. As described earlier, scripts have three main components: source files, script records, and script deployment records. From an auditing perspective, it is important to monitor all three components. Each component can be changed individually and have an impact on data integrity.

Source Files

For source files, a NetSuite saved search can be used to see all changes, including the date of the change and the user who made the change. These changes can then be tied back to a change management process. To view these changes, create a new search as outlined below:

1. Create a new saved search for the **Document** record type

New Saved Search

Contact

Customer

Deleted Record

Department

Document

Email Template

2. Add a new filter for the **File Type** field. Typically, script business logic will be contained in JavaScript files with a .js extension. However, it is possible that other file types are included in a script's execution. To limit the search to JavaScript files, add a filter for JavaScript File.

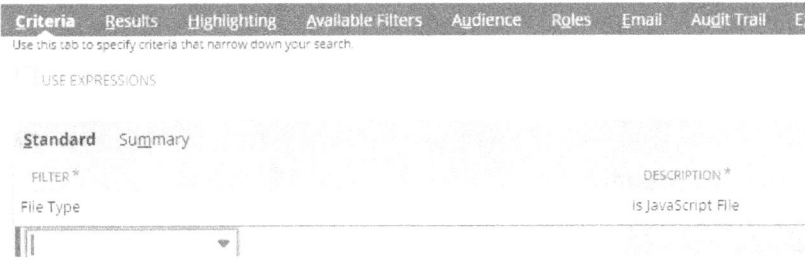

3. To see when the file was last changed and who made the change, add the following fields under the **Results** tab:
   - Name
   - Type (file type)

- System Notes: Date (when the change was made)
- System Notes: Set By (who made the change)

The results of the saved search will display the script file name, when it was last changed, and who changed the file.

 The process described above will identify changes made to source files but not provide details on the specific lines of code that were modified as part of the change. It is recommended to use a source control repository to determine specific lines of code that were modified as part of a release.

Script / Script Deployment Records

As of the 2016.2 release, both script and script deployment records support system notes. This is great news as system notes will provide field level details with old and new values along with the date of the change and the user who made the change. To view all changes made against scripts and script deployments records, create a new search as outlined below:

1. Create a new saved search for the **Script** or **Script Deployment** record type

New Saved Search

Quota

Report

Role

Saved Search

Scheduled Script Instance

Script

Script Deployment

Server Script Log

2. Add a filter for the System Notes **Record Type** field and set to the relevant record type, either script or script deployment. Without this filter, it is possible duplicate results or return irrelevant results. This is due to a bug that exists when running saved searches against script or script deployment records that include a join to system notes.

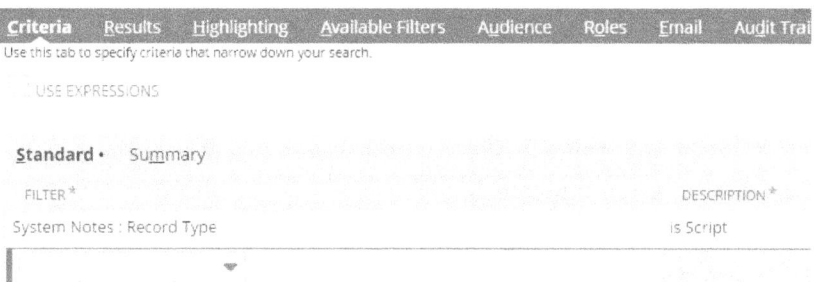

| Criteria | Results | Highlighting | Available Filters | Audience | Roles | Email | Audit Trai |

Use this tab to specify criteria that narrow down your search.

USE EXPRESSIONS

Standard · Summary

FILTER *   DESCRIPTION *

System Notes : Record Type   is Script

3. To see details about the changes made, add the following fields under the **Results** tab:

    *   Name
    *   System Notes: Context (where the change was made)
    *   System Notes: Date (when the change was made)
    *   System Notes: Field (field that was changed)

- System Notes: New Value (new value of the field as result of the change)
- System Notes: Old Value (old value of the field prior to the change)
- System Notes: Set by (who made the change)

The results of the saved search will show detailed changes against the script or script deployment records in the users NetSuite account.

SuiteTalk

SuiteTalk is the platform for interacting with NetSuite data programmatically through an XML-based application programming interface, otherwise known as an API (commonly referred to as web services in NetSuite). SuiteTalk provides a user interface in NetSuite for managing requests made through the API and the required schemas that developers can use to build properly formatted XML-based requests for interacting with NetSuite data.

The SuiteTalk API provides developers the ability to interact with data in NetSuite such as entities, transactions, and custom objects. Common actions taken through the SuiteTalk API include searching, creating, updating, and deleting records.

Security Model

Similar to a user logging into NetSuite through a web browser, web services rely on NetSuite's roles and permissions model. Every web services request must include credentials and specify a role. If no role is specified, the user's default role is used. The role used must have the web services permission to make web service requests. In addition to the permissions defined on the role, web service requests also respect any preferred custom forms. Attempting to set fields not available on preferred custom forms will result in an error.

To enhance web service integration security, NetSuite roles can be specified as Web Services Only. With this setting active, NetSuite will validate all requests made through the given role to ensure that each request is made from the context of web services and not from the user interface. This can be useful in scenarios in which a user's access through web services may differ from what that same user can access through the user interface.

Integration Management

Requests from external applications are controlled via one or more integration records in NetSuite. Integration records provide the ability to manage the state of the integration (whether the integration is enabled or not), view activity logs, and specify the available authentication methods. Integration records allow administrators to easily block requests coming from a specific application. Changes to integration records are tracked via system notes, making auditing of integration records straightforward.

Authentication

Every web service request must be authenticated prior to processing. NetSuite provides four methods of authentication for web service requests:

- User Credentials
- Token-Based Authentication
- Inbound Single Sign-on (Inbound SSO)
- Outbound Single Sign-on (SuiteSignOn)

User credential authentication requires an email address, password, role, and NetSuite account ID to be associated with each request. With user credential authentication, it is possible for web service requests to be made under the context of the Administrator role.

Token-based authentication is a standards-based authentication model that requires access tokens to be set up in NetSuite to provide authentication credentials. The combination of an integration record and an access token provides unique values known as the consumer key, consumer secret, token key, and token secret. These values, along with a NetSuite account ID, are required on every web service request made using token-based authentication. Overall integration security is improved with this approach as user credentials are no longer stored with the integrating application and token-based authentication cannot be used to log into the NetSuite user interface. With token-based authentication, requests cannot be made under the context of the Administrator role.

Inbound Single Sign-on, also referred to as Inbound SSO, is used to provide authentication to NetSuite based on authentication to an external application.

Outbound Single Sign-on, also referred to as SuiteSignOn, provides NetSuite users with access to external applications directly from the NetSuite user interface. In the context of web services, requests may be made back to NetSuite from the external application once SuiteSignOn authentication has been completed.

SuiteFlow

SuiteFlow is a collection of tools for managing workflow-based business processes in NetSuite. It consists of a user interface for authoring workflows, an engine for triggering or scheduling workflows, and administration tools for managing existing workflows. A workflow definition is attached to a specific record type and contains separate states for each step in a given business process. Each state contains actions, such as creating records or sending emails, and defines how the workflow transitions between other states in the process. An example workflow is illustrated below (using NetSuite's template for Journal Entry Basic Approval):

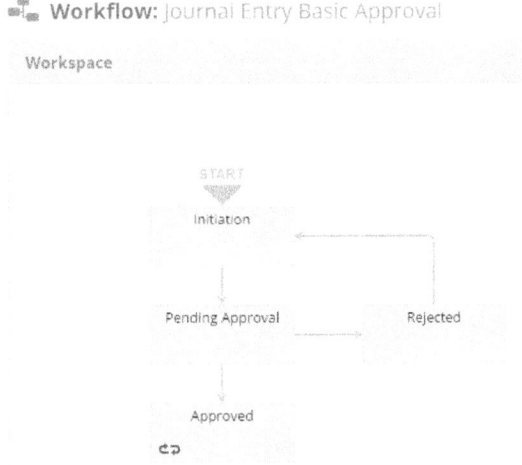

In this example, a NetSuite user creates a journal entry record, which triggers an instance of the approval workflow. The states and actions defined within the workflow then control how the journal entry progresses through the approval process.

161

From a security context, it is important to understand how a workflow audience is defined: users who can create and view workflow definitions and users who can run workflows.

To create and view workflows, a user must have either the Administrator role or the Workflow permission, which has a single access level of Full. However, having the Workflow permission is not enough. A user must also have Full Access to the base record specified in the workflow definition.

Workflows will run for users based on multiple criteria. First, the user must have access to the workflow base record and the appropriate access levels as required by the workflow. For example, if a workflow runs on Journal Entry records, a user must have access to the Journal Entry record for the workflow to be triggered for that user. Additionally, the user must have access to any joined records that are accessed via the workflow. For example, a workflow running on the Invoice record type may set field values on the customer associated with the invoice. In this case, the user must also have at least View permission to the Customer record type. Finally, workflows will only run for users if the workflow's Release Status is set to Released.

Execute as Admin

Workflows contain an Ex**ecute as Admin** setting that can override the role permissions for the user role that initiated the workflow instance. With this setting turned on, the workflow instance will run under the security context of the Administrator role, which means the workflow will have access to all records and actions available via SuiteFlow. The **Override Period Restrictions** permission is an exception to this rule. Even if the workflow is set to Execute as Admin, the user must still have the Override Period Restrictions permission in order to post transactions in locked periods. The Execute as Admin setting is only available to users who have the Administrator role.

Auditing

Like SuiteScript, SuiteFlow often plays a large role in an organization's business processes. It is important to have a grasp of who is modifying workflows and what they are changing. Unlike scripts and script deployments, workflows do not currently support system notes. This means we can only use saved searches to determine the last time a workflow was modified. From there, we will need to go into each individual workflow to identify changes. To determine which workflows have been changed, create a new search as outlined below:

1. Create a new saved search for the **Workflow** record type

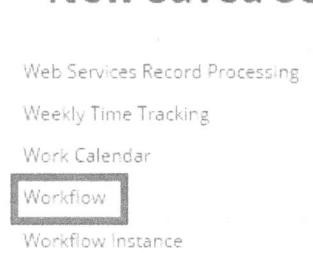

2. Add the following fields under the **Results** tab:
   - Name
   - Record Type (type of record workflow runs against)
   - Release Status (current release status of the workflow)
   - Date Modified (last date / time the workflow was modified)

The results of the saved search will show a listing of all workflows, including the last time they were modified.

163

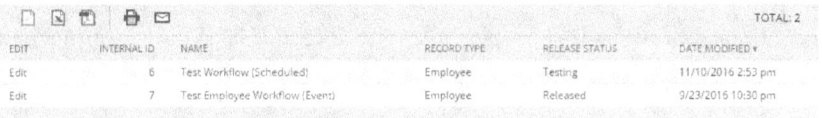

Now that we know which workflows were modified, we need to go into the details of each individual workflow to identify detailed changes.

1. Using the search results we generated above, click the **Edit** button next to the workflow to investigate further. This will open the workflow editor.

2. From here, click the pencil icon to display workflow details.

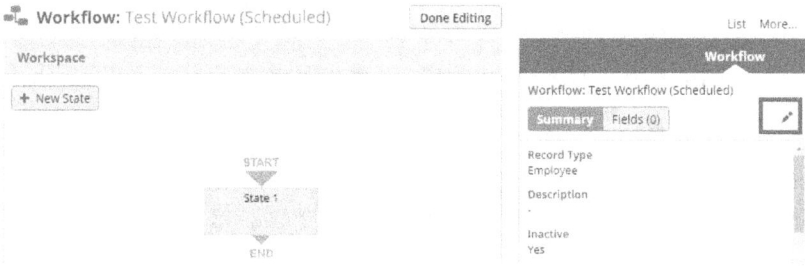

3. Once the workflow details have opened, navigate to the History subtab to see details of all changes made to the given workflow.

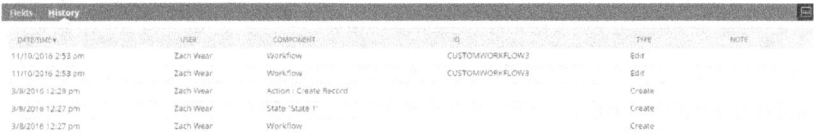

{7}

ADDITIONAL CONTROL CONSIDERATIONS

- Access Review and Certification
- Monitoring

This chapter addresses other control items that weren't previously covered or that need some extra emphasis. Backup and restore processes and security reporting are important monitoring activities. Security review is an often-overlooked activity and a key piece of access review and certification. We'll also tackle a couple of leftovers.

Principles

In addition to all the things we've looked at, there are a few other control items that are important, and we want to make sure we cover them.

Backup and Restore

A key, basic control is backing up and restoring ERP data. If everything goes wrong, being able to restore data is a last-ditch control. It's tough to deliver financial statements if system information is known to be wrong, and it's almost impossible if there's no information in the system.

In an ERP system maintained on premise, the responsibility for backing up, validating, and restoring information usually falls on the company's IT staff. However, the responsibility for the information contained in that ERP system belongs to the accounting team. This shared responsibility means that accounting can't simply defer responsibility and hope that the ERP system is being backed up. There must also be a process to test restoring information on regular basis.

Ideally, the backup and restore process should be part of a larger, documented disaster recovery plan that includes the company's risk tolerance for lost data and downtime. The key point here is testing the recovery. For many companies, a simple process is to periodically restore a backup of production to a test or development environment.

These environments are usually refreshed at some type of interval anyway, and restoring them from a scheduled backup is a way of validating the backup and restore process. Note that the restore shouldn't be done from backups made specifically for restoring to test. A process like that tests that a restore can be done, but it doesn't test that the regular backups work as designed.

In an online model, the responsibility for backup and restore usually rests with the provider. Again, though, there is a shared responsibility to ensure that the backup and restore process works as designed. It is important that the process, timing, and any limitations are completely understood. The process of restoring from a backup to a test environment also works well in an online model to ensure that backups can be restored.

Security Reviews

Security reviews are another important control consideration. Security reviews are just that – a review of many of the security controls we've already looked at. Security reviews include things like periodic reviews for orphaned users, access reviews, and segregation of duties monitoring. For a security review to be effective, issues and anomalies need to be investigated and either fixed or documented. For a security review to have taken place, there needs to be evidence, typically in the form of a report and a signature, electronic or physical. Without evidence that a review has been done, auditors are forced to conclude that the review did not occur.

Security Reports

Security reviews rely primarily on security reporting. These can be traditional reports, alerts, ad hoc reports, etc. Security reports can be delivered on a schedule or run manually; again, the key is that there is evidence of reviews.

Application

Backup and Restore

NetSuite's marketing message is heavy with information on their database reliability and redundancy. This includes information on disaster recovery and hot backups. NetSuite's systems are well designed to deal with large scale disasters, that is, those scenarios in which NetSuite would be responsible for data recovery. However,

NetSuite's Help is extremely thin on details of what to do in a disaster situation caused by the user organization.

For example, if an employee accidently, and incorrectly, changes a significant amount of information through an import or a mass update, what options are available to recover the original information? The best answer is to open a support case with NetSuite. There's no user accessible option to restore data, so it is important for firms to discuss this with NetSuite and understand their options.

There are some things that can be done. In the scenario described above, System Notes could be used to identify the changed data and develop a process to revert to the original information using Mass Modify or an export and reimport via CSV for example. Alternatively, correct information might be available in a sandbox environment, and the correct information could be exported from a sandbox and imported into the NetSuite production environment.

Sandbox

NetSuite does have a process to copy a production account to a sandbox environment, which is very handy for testing and development work, and very useful to help revert user errors. To access the sandbox settings:

1. A user MUST be in the production environment.
2. Navigate to **Setup > Company > Company Management Sandbox Accounts.**

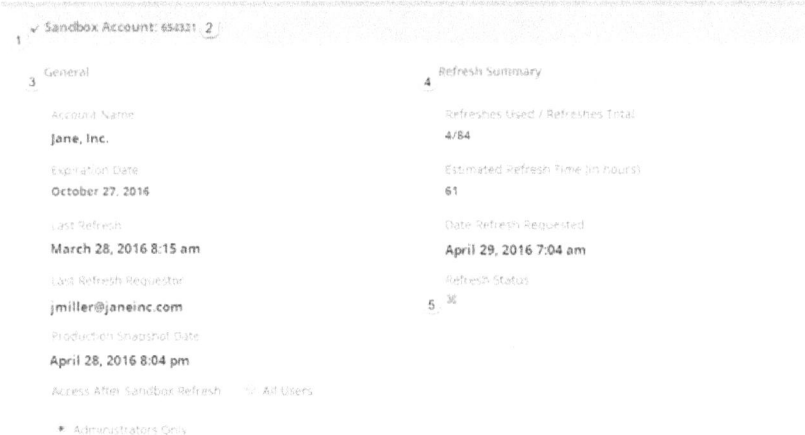

The NetSuite Help topic **Using the Sandbox Accounts Page**[10] explains the related sections.

Legend
1. Account Status is displayed to the left of the Sandbox Account heading.
2. The Account ID (scompid) is displayed to the right of the Sandbox Account heading.
3. General account information.
4. Refresh Summary information.
5. The Refresh Status indicator is displayed here.

Account Status is shown to the left of the Sandbox Account ID. Applicable account statuses are:

- **Online:** A green check.
- **Offline:** An empty circle. The account is not available for use. A sandbox being refreshed will display this status until the refresh process is complete.
- **Expired:** a red X. The account was not renewed as of the expiration date and is no longer available for use.

The General Account information window displays:

---

[10] NetSuite, NetSuite Help "Using the Sandbox Accounts Page" NetSuite.com (November 2016)

- **Sandbox Account** - Name of sandbox account.
- **Expiration Date** - Date the sandbox account is scheduled to expire.
- **Last Refresh** - Date when the most recent refresh of the sandbox account was completed.
- **Last Refresh Requestor** - User who requested the most recent refresh.
- **Production Snapshot Date** - Date and time of the production snapshot used for the most recent refresh. The backup copy is taken from the night before the sandbox refresh starts. This date may not be the same as the date the refresh was requested or the date it was completed. (Note that the time is formatted based on the current user's Time Format preference, set at Home > Set Preferences.)
- **Access After Sandbox Refresh** - Companies can choose to provide default account access to all users or only to administrators after the refresh. The selection made remains in effect for subsequent refreshes unless its changed.
- **All Users** - If this option is selected, after the refresh access can be removed from users as needed.

 Customer Center roles are not copied during sandbox refreshes. Even if the option is selected to give all users access after the refresh, users assigned the Customer Center role are excluded from this access. Because of this limitation, customer login functionality does not work in a sandbox after a refresh, even if it has been working in the production account. To set up this functionality to work in a sandbox, perform a CSV import of customer records into the sandbox account to set passwords and set Give Access to True for customer users.

- **Administrators Only** - If this option is selected, after the refresh, access can be added to users as needed.

 Only the Administrator role is copied to the sandbox. That is, for a user with multiple roles, only the Administrator role for that user is copied to the sandbox.

The Refresh Summary section contains:

- **Refreshes Used / Refreshes Total** - Number of refreshes used out of the total number of refreshes available. For companies with multiple sandbox accounts, the refresh count is shared between all the sandbox accounts.

- **Estimated Refresh Time** - Estimated number of hours required for the refresh to complete. (Note that this estimate is not exact.)

- **Date Refresh Requested** - Date and time when the most recent refresh was requested.

- **Refresh Status** - Status of the most recent refresh. When a refresh fails, a popup error message displays. This message includes an error ticket number that as user can provide to Customer Support to help them resolve the issue. When the production account and the sandbox account are not running the same version, a red x displays, and a popup version mismatch error displays.

The sandbox process has several refresh statuses. These include:

- **Awaiting Processing**: The refresh request has been submitted and will be processed in the order received.
- **Pending Copy to Sandbox** This notice only appears for newly provisioned sandboxes. Administrators can choose when to initiate the copy of data from the production account to the sandbox.
- The **Copy Data to Sandbox** button only appears on the Sandbox Accounts page of newly provisioned sandboxes.
- Click **Copy Data to Sandbox** to initiate the copy of data from the associated production account. The sandbox status will not change to online until the copy of data is completed. (After the initial data copy to the sandbox has completed, the **Refresh Sandbox** button is displayed on the Sandbox Accounts page.)
- **Delayed**: The refresh progress has been delayed. There are occasions when the refresh estimate prediction software initially assigns the Delayed status to a refresh request. If a sandbox status is set to Delayed before entering Refresh in Progress, access to the existing sandbox is maintained until the status changes to Refresh in Progress. If the refresh request is in Delayed status, an Administrator can check the Sandbox Accounts page to verify whether the existing sandbox is still online and accessible.
- **Refresh In Progress**: The sandbox refresh is ongoing.
- **Refresh Failed**: An error occurred during the refresh process. NetSuite Customer Support will intervene to help resolve the problem. When a refresh fails, a popup error message displays. This message includes an error ticket number that a user can provide to NetSuite Customer Support to help them resolve the issue. The Refresh Failed status can also be reported when the

172

sandbox and the production account are running different versions of NetSuite software. This can occur during the new release period, when the production account has been upgraded, but the sandbox has not yet been upgraded to the new release.

- **Complete**: The sandbox refresh process is complete, and the sandbox account status is online and accessible.

The **Refresh Sandbox** button on the Sandbox Accounts page is used to request a refresh of a sandbox account.

 A refresh completely replaces the content of the sandbox account with the content of the production account. After a sandbox account has been refreshed from production, it cannot be restored to its prior state. Before submitting a request to refresh a sandbox account, please ensure that company users are fully notified and ready for the refresh from production. The refresh request cannot be cancelled or otherwise modified in any way after it has been accepted.

For new sandbox accounts, a copy of data from the associated production account needs to be initiated by clicking the **Copy Data to Sandbox** button. This action must be completed before a new sandbox account comes online. The Refresh Sandbox and Copy Data buttons are not available unless both the sandbox and its associated production accounts are running the same version of NetSuite.

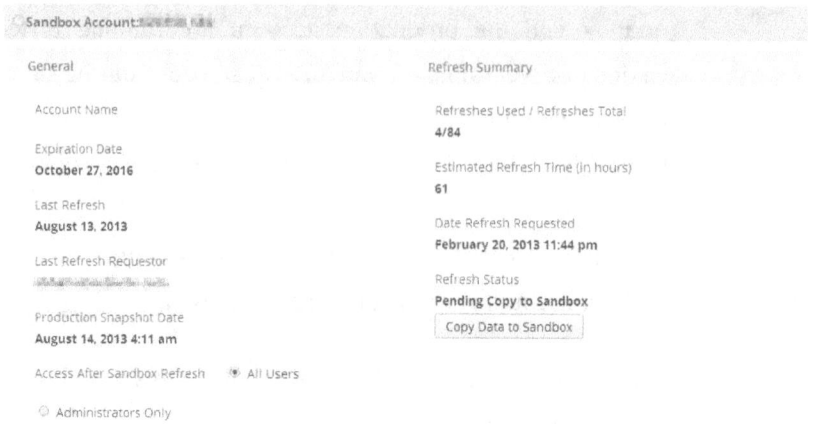

NetSuite's Help file has lots of additional information on setting up and using sandbox environments.

Security Reviews and Reporting

We've already spent some time with the Saved Search feature in NetSuite and it's going to be the backbone of security reviews in NetSuite. Some common searches that can be saved and used in security reviews include:

- List of enabled users
- User with sensitive or critical access
- Privileged user access
- Login audit trail
- Roles assigned to users
- Terminations
- Deleted transactions
- Transaction line changes
- Journal entry changes
- Financial reports changes
- Configuration changes

Some critical items, like segregation of duties, can be difficult and time consuming to review via NetSuite searches. Also, we've covered sign-off for reviews at length in the principles section, but NetSuite doesn't provide a good mechanism for electronic signatures on reports. That is something that will need to be addressed with a policy that could include physical reviews and signatures or a third-party option like Assure from Fastpath.

 Fastpath Assure includes a prebuilt, customizable segregation of duties rule set combined with SoD conflict analysis to make analyzing segregations of duties much easier. Additionally, Assure's access review reporting can reduce the number of saved searches that need to be created and keep access reviews all in one place. Finally, Assure facilitates electronic signatures for security reviews making it easy to provide evidence of ongoing reviews.

{8}

AUDITING NETSUITE

- Monitoring

Auditing is all about monitoring and validating that controls are working properly. We took a little different approach to this chapter, but we think it's important.

Principles

While this book is primarily about setting up and managing security in NetSuite, auditing is an important part of validating that security and controls are working as designed.

Auditing

We won't spend a ton of time on auditing principles. So much has been written about auditing principles that we could never even recap it all in this book. We're using the term auditing a bit generically here in that the audit in question could be an external audit that is focused on the integrity of financial statements, it could be an internal audit geared toward process improvement or segregation of duties, or something as simple as monitoring the effectiveness of specific controls.

We suspect that readers who are more audit focused might skip over other chapters and come directly here. Because of that, we've built in some overlap with items covered in other chapters, but we think it's helpful to have these items grouped together in a single chapter, even if some basic information is repeated. The application steps may be a little shorter too, as we aren't going to go quite as deep for these items. Know that many of these items are covered in greater depth throughout the book. Finally, this isn't an exhaustive list of audit tools and options, but we tried to hit the big stuff.

Application

System Notes

The **System Notes** feature tracks data and configuration changes including the date when the change was made, the user who made the change, the type of change, along with the old and new values. System notes track changes on both custom records and standard records. Users with View access to a record can view the system notes for that record. System notes are typically found under the **Information** subtab for a record.

System note searches are available for specific records, can be used with advanced search filters, can be used as part of a saved search, and can be exported for additional analysis.

It's important to understand that system notes don't quite track everything, but they come pretty close. We cover system notes in more detail in the Audit Trail section of Chapter 5.

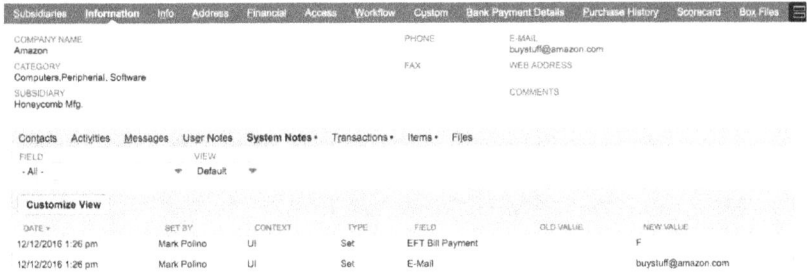

Audit Trails

Audit trails are searches of system notes with predefined filters and results. Since these are based on system notes, almost all financial transactions are tracked and searchable. Access to audit trails can be found on a **Transaction List** page in the upper right or by navigating to **Transactions > Management > View Audit Trail**.

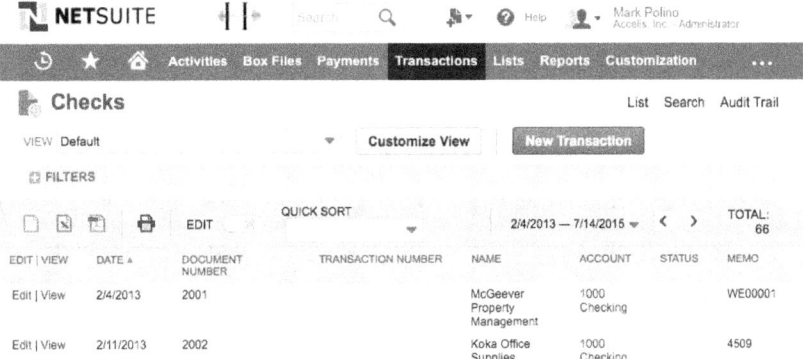

Since an audit trail is just a report on system notes, it provides the same information in a consolidated place.

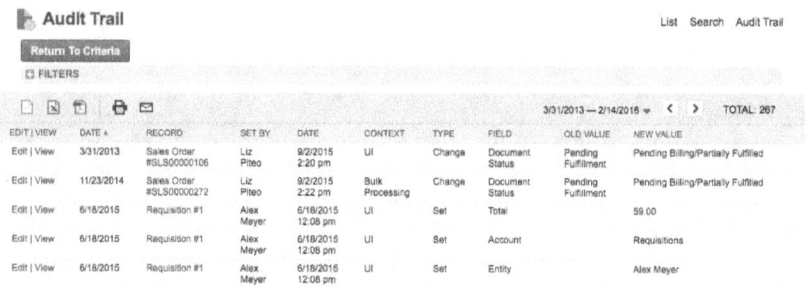

Tracked vs. Searchable

Before we get deeper into tools to help with auditing NetSuite, it's important to understand tracked information versus searchable information.

Financial changes can be tracked and displayed via:

- System Notes subtab
- Audit Trail link
- History subtab

System Notes and Audit Trails are the results of searches of the System Notes table. Some pages, like configuration pages, don't have a system notes tab or an Audit Trail link. Instead users can create a saved search with their own criteria, filters, and results.

History subtabs are not searchable.

Search of record types that support system notes can include system note details in their results. For example, a customer search can include system note field values related to customer record changes by using Personalize Search.

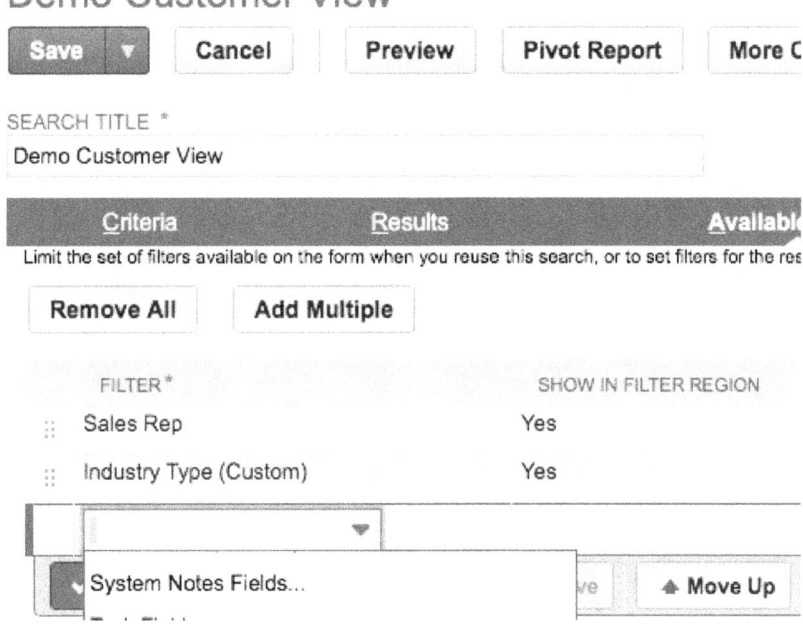

Contexts

Finally, before we move on, users can also include a Context field in a system notes search to identify how the change was made. For example, the Context field can show if a change was made via a mass update, through the mobile app, or via scripting.

Context is included by default in Audit Trail reports but may need to be added in other reporting.

EDIT | VIEW	DATE ▲	RECORD	SET BY	DATE	CONTEXT
Edit | View	3/31/2013	Sales Order #SLS00000106	Liz Piteo	9/2/2015 2:20 pm	UI
Edit | View	11/23/2014	Sales Order #SLS00000272	Liz Piteo	9/2/2015 2:22 pm	Bulk Processing
Edit | View	6/18/2015	Requisition #1	Alex Meyer	6/18/2015 12:08 pm	UI

Transaction Audit Trail

A Transaction Audit Trail report allows users to produce a report that provides a detailed history of transactions entered into NetSuite. To produce this report:

1. Select **Transactions > Management > View Audit Trail.**
2. On the **View Audit Trail** page, filter the report by:
    a. Users
    b. Action
    c. Date
    d. Amount
    e. Transaction Type
    f. Account
    g. Name

View Audit Trail

3. Click **Submit.**

The resulting report will have transaction details including:

- Date/Time the transaction was executed
- Username of the individual who made the change
- Action taken
- Type of transaction
- Internal ID
- Document number
- Posting date of the transaction
- Amount

Audit Trail

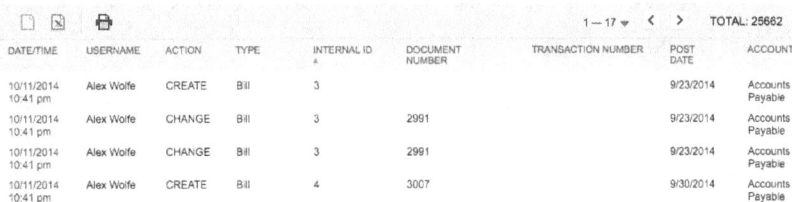

Deleted Transactions

NetSuite retains some information about deleted records. This information can be retrieved using the **Deleted Record** search type.

To use this search type:
1. Go to **Reports > New Search**.
2. Click **Deleted Record.**
3. Set **Criteria**.
4. Click **Submit**.

By default, the Deleted Records permission is only assigned to the Administrator and Full Access role.

Administration & Controls Tool Kit (ACT) SuiteSolution

The Administration and Controls Tool Kit (ACT) is a SuiteSolution available for purchase from NetSuite. ACT provides a set of additional tools managing access, security, and internal controls. ACT includes enhanced features for administration and control including:

- Risk and compliance dashboard.
  - o Searches on system notes of scripts and configuration items.
  - o Searches for role and permission changes, including the ability to tag certain roles as relevant.
- Delete record tracker/prevention.
- Employee role removal automation with alerts.
- Automatic termination of access to production and sandbox and across environments.
- SuiteScript directory and file locking.
- Temporary access to locked script directory and files.

Transaction Line Changes

Audit Trails can be viewed for individual line items directly from each transaction record's listing for items, expenses, and journal line items. To view transaction line changes on a journal entry as an example:

1. Find a Journal Entry using **Transactions > Financial > Make Journal Entries > List** (or **Search**).
2. Click **View** next to the journal entry.
3. Select a line and click the **History** link for that line.

A blank line indicates no history. Effectively, this means no changes; the line is the original entry. History appears if there have been changes to the line.

Transaction level history can be exported to CSV or Excel using the buttons just above the History lines.

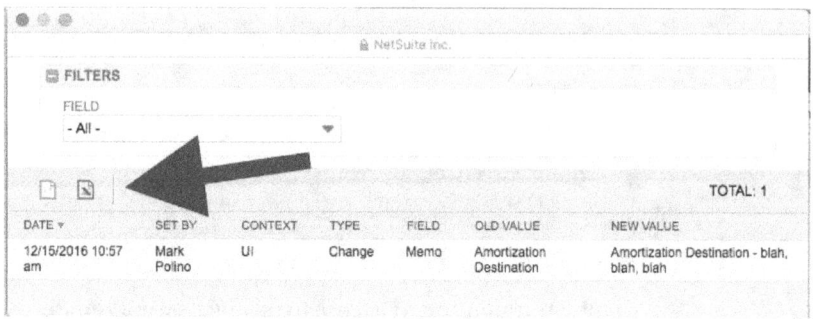

Commonly Audited Items

Revenue Recognition – For companies using Revenue Recognition in NetSuite, changes to Revenue Arrangements, Revenue Elements, Revenue Recognition Rules, and Revenue Recognition plans can be tracked via System Notes.

Items and Projects – The Items and Projects list pages include an Audit Trail link. Each item and project record also includes a System Information subtab with system notes, active workflows, and a history of workflows executed against the item.

Journal Entries – Each journal entry includes a System Information subtab with system notes, a list of active workflows, and a history of workflow executed against that journal entry.

Configuration Changes – Changes to general configuration changes that can have a financial impact are logged in system notes for:
- Company information

- General preferences
- Accounting lists
- Tax setup

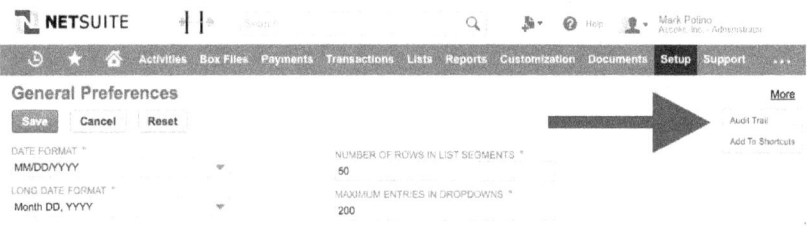

Financial Reports

An **Analytics Audit Trail** can be used to display audit trail data with changes to the definitions of saved searches, custom reports, report schedules, and financial report layouts. Analytics Audit Trail searches are covered in detail in Chapter 5, but here is a short recap on how to use them:

1. Go to **Reports > New Search**.
2. Click **Analytics Audit Trail**.
3. Use the **Record Type** list to specify the record types to be included in the search.
4. To refine a search further, use the following fields:
   a. **Date** – For changes during a specific time period, enter the time period.
   b. **From/To** – Enter the start and end dates for the period.
   c. **Component Name** – For changes to a specific search or report component, enter the name of the component.
   d. **Component Type** – For changes to search or report components of a specific type, enter this type.

e. **Component Action** – For a specific action that resulted in changes, enter this action.

f. The **Old Value** and **New Value** fields can be used to look for specific values before or after the change.

5. Click **Submit** to see the changes, or **Create Saved Search** to create a saved search based on the criteria.

6. For Analytics Audit Trails, once a financial report with changes has been identified, navigate to the report in NetSuite and use **More Options > Audit Trail** to see the specific changes.

Use a prefix like "FIN" in front of custom financial reports makes it easy to identify them in an audit trail.

Audit Sampling

NetSuite has functionality to make audit sampling easier. A report can be scheduled and emailed to auditors as a CSV file on a regular basis. Data is pulled directly from NetSuite so there is a single source of truth. Audit reports can be sent ahead of time and gather automatically, meaning there is no need for lists of prepared-by-client (PBC) documents.

Additionally, reports run in NetSuite provide full functionality to drill down on report results, all the way down to the transaction level. When running a report or saved search, clicking on entity names, transaction numbers, or amounts provides drill down to the records, transaction, or a detail report.

Common Reports for Audit

Common finance reports for audit include:

- Trial Balance
- Open Purchase Orders
- Paid Employee Commission
- Deferred Revenue Rollforward
- Unrealized Exchange Rate Gains & Losses
- AR Aging

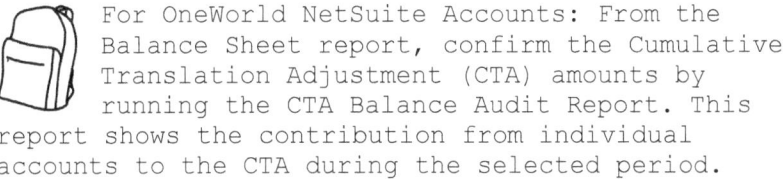 For OneWorld NetSuite Accounts: From the Balance Sheet report, confirm the Cumulative Translation Adjustment (CTA) amounts by running the CTA Balance Audit Report. This report shows the contribution from individual accounts to the CTA during the selected period.

Benchmarking

Benchmarking or baselining should be used initially on configurations and system-generated reports. Once settings are in place, generate a report with this baseline information. Then change management controls can be used to provide alerts on changes to the automated controls.

For configurations, the System Notes saved search alerts for the relevant configuration pages can be used to determine if changes have been made.

For customized reports, the Analytics Audit saved search alert can be used to identify changes to compare them to the benchmarked version.

KPIs, Graphs, and Smart Dashboards

NetSuite provides a prebuilt set of Key Performance Indicators (KPIs) that may be helpful for auditing NetSuite. Custom KPIs can also be built to address other needs that aren't included in the prebuilt set.

Additionally, NetSuite's trend graphs may be used when analyzing data as part of an audit or audit preparation. KPIs and other elements can be added to a smart dashboard providing easy and consistent access to data.

KPIs, graphs, and Smart Dashboards are detailed in NetSuite Help. These can be great tools to understand changes in NetSuite, but they are bit more than what we want to detail in this book.

Fastpath Tools

Fastpath Assure provides a comprehensive audit solution to automate risk management and Sarbanes-Oxley compliance for NetSuite. This includes segregation of duties analysis using an easily customizable, out-of-the-box rule set to quickly analyze security conflicts within and across roles. Also included is additional security analysis, simple sign-off for mitigations, and scheduled report delivery. Assure for NetSuite's audit trail features enhance NetSuite's System Notes reporting capability and provides point-in-time snapshots to help identify changes to NetSuite metadata and other fields not tracked via System Notes. Finally, Identity Manager from Fastpath delivers workflow-based provisioning for NetSuite users with SoD conflict analysis, including editing and terminating NetSuite users, along with user, role, and global permission level effective dates.

SUMMARY

Security is an important consideration in any financial system and NetSuite is no exception. NetSuite provides a wealth of security options and tools to help companies establish a secure control environment. In addition to NetSuite's built-in tools, additional applications, like Fastpath Assure, provide an important supplement to NetSuite's governance, risk, and compliance capabilities.

Ultimately no software can perfectly secure a working environment. Companies are responsible for implementing a complete control environment including appropriate controls, segregation of duties, and taking a risk-based approach to the process.

In this book, we've tried to highlight the principles underlying good security and explain how to apply those principles to a NetSuite environment. A book can't address every situation, but we hope that we've helped with the most common and relevant ones. As we've referenced earlier, NetSuite's Help documentation provides a wealth of information to address scenarios that go beyond this book. Additionally, Fastpath provides a wealth of tools designed to help companies address their security, audit, and compliance needs in NetSuite.

EDITION NOTE

Since NetSuite is cloud based, it's relatively easy for them to provide updates to the entire NetSuite user base. Typically, NetSuite releases two updates a year and moves users to each new update pretty aggressively. This is a problem for NetSuite books. Without regular updates, book content gets stale. Is a book written for NetSuite in 2011 really still relevant?

Because of this we're making a commitment to update this book with each NetSuite release. Our editions are numbered in conjunction with NetSuite's numbering system. This edition is 2017.2 to correspond with the 2017.2 NetSuite release. If we have to make a significant change in the book prior to the next NetSuite release, we'll number the new release 2017.2 Mk1. The Mk1 fits nicely with the field manual theme and indicates a book change, not a NetSuite change.

Some releases may not have much in the way of security changes, while others could see significant rework. NetSuite continues to reduce the security areas that require Administrator access so there is ongoing security work. With a topic as important as security and audit, we feel it's important to keep up to date.

You can find additional information at:
www.gofastpath.com/netsuitebook.

INDEX